VINTAGE TYPE & GRAPHICS

An ECLECTIC COLLECTION OF TYPOGRAPHY, ORNAMENT, LETTERHEADS, And TRADEMARKS FROM 1896–1936

ALLWORTH PRESS
NEW YORK

ALLWORTH PRESS
NEW YORK

VINTAGE TYPE AND GRAPHICS

Includes All Images URL

An ECLECTIC COLLECTION OF YPOGRAPHY, ORNAMENT, ETTERHEADS, And TRADEMARKS FROM 896–1936

STEVEN HELLER & LOUISE FILI

ACKNOWLEDGMENTS

The authors are indebted to Mary Jane Callister of Louise Fili, Ltd., for her tasteful design and devoted oversight of thi project. Thanks also to John Passafiume for his meticulous work on the cover design.

This would not be possible if not for our editors at Allworth Press. We are grateful to Delia Casa and Jamie Kijowsk associate editors, Nicole Potter, editor, Bob Porter, associate publisher, and of course, Tad Crawford, publisher, wh supports and encourages a wide range of graphic design publishing.

Thanks also to our favorite antiquarian booksellers for providing the lion's share of material from which we compiled thi book. Irving and Lenore Oaklander, Oaklander Books, New York; Robert and Dorothy Emerson, R&D Emerson Book Falls Village, Connecticut; and David Batterham, David Batterham Books, London, England.

SH & LF

 All inquiries should be addressed to Allworth Press, 30 West 36th Street, 11th Floor, New York, NY 10018. Allworth Press books may be purchased in bulk at special discounts for sales promo tion, corporate gifts, fund-raising, or educational purposes. Special editions can also be created to specifications. For details, contact th Special Sales Department, Allworth Press, 307 West 36th Street, 11th Floor, New York, NY 10018 or info@skyhorsepublishing.com 23 22 21 9 8 7 Published by Allworth Press, an imprint of Skyhorse Publishing, Inc. 307 West 36th Street, 11th Floor, New Yor NY 10018. Allworth Press® is a registered trademark of Skyhorse Publishing, Inc.®, a Delaware corporation. www.allworth.com Interior design by Louise Fili Ltd. Page composition/typography by Mary Jane Callister / Louise Fili Ltd. An earlier edition of this boo was previously published under the title: *Design Connoisseur: An Eclectic Collection of Imagery and Type*. Library of Congress Cataloging-in-Publication Data is available on file. ISBN: 978-1-58115-892-2. Printed in China.

Materials from this book are available for download on the Skyhorse website.
Navigate to the book's detail page here: skyhorsepublishing.com/go/9781581158922
Download the materials from the Links section.

INTRODUCTION

THE VINTAGE FETISHIST

"VINTAGE" MAKES TYPE SOUND LIKE A RARE WINE. FOR GRAPHIC DESIGNERS, TYPE IS INDEED LIKE TRULY FINE WINE, TO BE savored as such. Nonetheless, we would have been willing to call this book "Design Fetish," since we are not connoisseurs per se, but fetishists, and collecting these "objects" of graphic design is indeed fetishistic. We love the look, feel, and even the moldy smell of this ephemera, and possess an enduring passion for commercial art's artifacts, especially the type books, trade magazines, and specimen sheets of the late nineteenth and early twentieth centuries that promoted graphic arts to the trade. They are abundant with the stuff that appeals to the aesthetic cravings of all designers. To call ourselves "connoisseurs" as opposed to "fetishists" would suggest a serious, if not also scholarly, interest in these objects as building blocks of an arcane history, when in truth, our obsession with them began more viscerally than intellectually. Finding a rare copy of a Deberny & Peignot type catalog, for example, or a run of *Das Plakat*, the German poster magazine, is like stumbling upon a Picasso canvas. In the hierarchy of art, the former may be of little consequence, but for collectors like us it is infinitely more valuable. Perspective is everything.

The word "fetish" has certain connotations of its own. So this book, with its more neutral "vintage" title, is a concession to our publisher, who would rather not have it mistakenly shelved in a bookstore's "Sexual How-To" section, nor banned in the Bible Belt as salacious. However, we hope that the book will not be placed in the "Cooking" or "Wine" sections, either.

Nonetheless, the word "vintage" is apt for our purposes. What began as a fetish has evolved into a kind of connoisseurship of the vintage in the art historical sense of the term. The content of this book is a veritable custodianship and study of significant objects that are endemic to understanding a particular art form. The graphic design ephemera collected on these pages has been used for two distinct purposes: as source material on which contemporary graphic design is often based; and as documentary material from which graphic design history is continually researched. The past is, as Tom Wolfe once noted, "A Big Closet," from which to draw inspiration and influence. Thus the art of graphic design—the development of form and concept—is rooted in the understanding of, if not physically borrowing from, historical materials. Yet in a field that grew out of services to business (i.e., sign painting and advertising) and was dependent on prevailing fashion and trend, few, if any, scholars saw the need to chronicle graphic design history. The written record from the past was, for the most part, created by practitioners and journalists writing for professional publications that addressed technical concerns and timely styles. Most of the text found in these publications is too rarefied to be of use even to historians. But design is a visual art, and the physical artifacts that were left behind—those items that were once viewed as temporary—are graphic design history's Lascaux Caves. The alphabets, advertisements, ornaments, letterheads, and marks presented in this book should be considered a body of evidence that links us to the past while it serves as a touchstone for the present.

Obviously, this book does not pretend to be a scholarly history. There is little text and no analysis of the visual material. Every example is reproduced as it appeared in its original context. And yet there is no attempt to offer definitive information regarding those contexts. While we have selected material spanning the late nineteenth and early twentieth centuries, it has not been organized in a chronological sequence, but rather according to how the respective objects are tied together through visual relationships. So, you might ask, what is the virtue of this collection? The answer is: critical mass.

This is our public "scrap file." Actually, we refer to it as raw material. All of it comes from rare antiquarian books, journals, and brochures in our libraries. Much of it has been previously referred to in some form or other in our respective graphic designs and historical research. These are but a few of the items, among thousands, that have helped our exploration of vintage practices. And these are some of the alphabets, decorative borders, initial caps, and stock clichés that comprised the earliest language of graphic design (and some that are still as viable as when they were originally created).

What is the purpose of collecting these artifacts in a book? Apart from the critical mass, we want to share the riches, so to speak, that have fueled our work. This is a portion of what has taken us almost two decades to accumulate, but individually and as a whole it has untold meaning. It is proof of a singular obsession. But unlike collecting tinfoil, bicycle seats, or rubber products, this preoccupation has certain benefits for the design culture in which we practice. By excerpting these items from lost and forgotten publications, and making these materials available in an unfettered way in an accessible volume, we hope to inspire others much in the same way that we have been inspired. How the book and downloadable content are ultimately used—as documentary or clip art, to savor or utilize—is not within our power to dictate. But for those who are totally unfamiliar, this is a bountiful sampling of historic material. For those who are already connoisseurs or fetishists of these vintage works, there is a trove of extraordinary, and extraordinarily rare, relics herein.

Our organization is consistent with graphic arts genres found in the type catalogs, sample books, and specimen sheets published between 1896 and 1936 from which the material was excerpted. The most voluminous section is "Typography," followed by "Ornament," both of which were mainstays of all hot metal type foundry businesses. Two smaller sections on "Letterheads" and "Trademarks" fill out the fundamental needs of the graphic designer and job printer (who often included design services as a loss-leader to attract business). The materials come from the United States, England, France, Germany, Italy, Spain, and Holland. Often the specimen book that originated in one country was modified for another. We tried to select samples that were unique to the country of origin. The titles and identification on the original pages were left in to provide some contextual grounding. But it is clear from looking at this material that despite some national and regional visual "dialects," the styles of type and ornament are fairly uniform.

You may consider our vintage collection as a reference, resource, or voyeuristic glimpse into an obsession in progress. You are free to actively use or passively enjoy the material. We hope, however, that whatever the book's ultimate function, it will serve as a wellspring of a relatively unknown past. Maybe it will also inspire you to become a fetishist too.

TYPOGRAPHY

TYPE IS A TOOL OF COMMUNICATION AND AN ART OF COMMERCE. THE FACT THAT IT IS AT ONCE FUNCTIONALLY enduring and aesthetically sublime is what has made type such a popular object of connoisseurship among those both in and out of the graphic design fields. Originally, letterforms were created to spread the Word, but ultimately, they were designed and redesigned to convey more quotidian ideas, many of which are sales pitches. The diversely styled alphabets presented in foundry-type specimen books dating back to the turn of the century had one purpose: Attract the eye. This does not mean that the respective designers did not view themselves as artisans of the highest magnitude. It simply meant that type, while still the means of spreading the Word, was also a device for establishing mood, aura, and style. In literature and official documents, it is enough that a typeface is readable. In advertising, however, which is the main market for typefaces produced by the major type foundries, a face must also have a distinct personality that demands attention.

The alphabets and specimens displayed here are not the classic typefaces that have endured centuries of stylistic and technological change. Rather, these gothics, scripts, swashes, and spiked letters are fashions of particular moments in time. They are the graphic arts equivalent of the Victorian bonnet, flapper's frock, and dandy's spats; the bastardizations, transfigurations, and novelizations of letters into objects of desire. Some are absurdly delightful; others are delightfully grotesque. All contain the proper number of characters and are completely functional.

INDÉPENDANT

No. 2553 Corps 96/72 4 A, 10 a Minimum 22 Kg.

De Boeken

No. 2552 Corps 72/60 5 A, 12 a Minimum 18 Kg.

Indépendant!

No. 2551 Corps 60/48 7 A, 15 a Minimum 16 Kg.

Krieg im Frieden

No. 2550 Corps 48/36 8 A, 22 a Minimum 14 Kg.

Sierkunst

No. 2549 Corps 36 8 A, 22 a Minimum 12 Kg.

Specie lijnen

DE BINDER

No. 2548 Corps 28 12 A, 30 a Minimum 10 Kg.

Steam Traction

NEIGHBOURS

ABCD

EFGHIJKL

MNOPQRST

UVWXYZ&

abcdefghijkl

mnopqrstuv

wxyz.,;:'!?-)

1234567890

N. V. LETTERGIETERIJ „AMSTERDAM" VOORHEEN N. TETTERODE

Cic. 15 - Classe C-a

Serie LUBECCA

BONI

MUTE

Cic. 16 - Classe C-c

BENE

A NEW
EUROPE

MOTORING
ABROAD
RAYMOND AND
WHITCOMB CO

GUERLAIN

EVERY SKIN LOOKS BETTER
WITH THE FINEST FILM
OF POWDER OVER IT.
AND EVERY HAT IS MORE
BECOMING IF THAT POW-
DER HAS A RICH AND
WARM COLOR. FOR
THESE REASONS
WE RECOMMEND
"LA POUDRE"
"C'EST"
"MOI"

EXHIBITION

YOU ARE CORDIALLY INVITED TO VIEW THE EXTRAORDINARY MODERN CONCEPTIONS OF THE PIANO, CREATED BY LEE SIMONSON, HELEN DRYDEN AND EDWARD J. STEICHEN, KNOWN AS THE

THESE AMAZING, TRULY MODERN PIANOS EXECUTED BY AMERICA'S LEADING MODERN ARTISTS ARE NOW ON EXHIBITION AT OUR SHOW-ROOMS, 433 FIFTH AVENUE, NEW YORK

HARDMAN · PECK & CO.

norris frank in

water snow yr

king queens in

arabesque abc

Cic. 4 - Classe A-h

Serie CUNEO

Corriere Mordace

VIA MODERNA

Cic. 5 - Classe A-i

Arte Novella

FUTURISMO

Cic. 6 - Classe A-l

Maschera 5

MENEGHIN

Serie CUNEO

Cic. 35 - Classe E-m — Cic. 40 - Classe F-m
Cic. 45 - Classe G-n — Cic. 60 - Classe I-p
Cic. 80 - Classe L-q — Cic. 100 - Classe M-l

Cic. 50 - Classe H-l

Now that sans serif types have attained a definite position in modern typography, it is well to examine the merits of each particular face from a design standpoint.

FUTURA

the type of today and tomorrow, lays just claim to being the soundest of all sans serif faces. Futura has no prototype. Its forms have been developed strictly in accordance with their function. It is an interpretation of the modern spirit. It is free of all eccentricities. It shows the same abstract qualities as modern architecture, automobiles and airplanes. Yet withal, its designer, Paul Renner, did not forget to embody the results of the latest scientific investigations to make it the most legible of all modern types. Futura is the first letter scientifically avoiding color vibration. Lights and darks are equally distributed. For color gradation it is presented in three different weights—light, medium and bold. Compare Futura with other sans serif letters; the differences are self-evident. We will gladly send specimen sheets for such comparisons. Futura, cast to the American point system, is available from 8 to 84 point in job fonts, and also in weight fonts from 8 to 18 point.

THE BAUER TYPE FOUNDRY · INC

235-247 EAST 45TH STREET · NEW YORK CITY

The Century...The Broadway...The Overland...The Golden State...Four of the dozens of superb trains operated daily over American Railroads. • To express these four and their many sisters, in type as powerful, as clean cut, as distinguished as the trains themselves, has hitherto been rather a problem. • With FUTURA BOLD, however, conveying the same energetic, abstract and logical qualities, this problem fades to the vanishing point. • Never was there a type face better suited to present the message of not only the railroads but also the entire heavy industries, than this...

FUTURA

the type of today and tomorrow

THE BAUER TYPE FOUNDRY, INC., NEW YORK

At Two-Thirty-Five East Forty-Fifth Street

Cic. 4 - Classe A-c

Serie DANIMARCA

ARTE XILOGRAFICA

CARATTERI LEGNO

Cic. 16 - Classe B-b — Cic. 35 - Classe D-b
Cic. 40 - Classe D-o — Cic. 45 - Classe F-c

Cic. 5 - Classe A-d

ORNAMENTALE

STILI MODERNI

Cic. 50 - Classe G-e — Cic. 60 - Classe H-q
Cic. 80 - Classe L-i — Cic. 100 - Classe M-d

Cic. 6 - Classe A-e

IL FUTURISMO

ARTISTICO 43

Cic. 12 - Classe A-n

Serie DANIMARCA

Cic. 18 - Classe B-c

Cic. 20 - Classe B-f

Lucio Ridenti

LA VITA GAIA DI DINA GALLI

ROMANZO BIOGRAFICO

COPERTINA DI
*** CARBONI ***

Se questo romanzo della mia vita l'avessi scritto io non sarebbe riuscito più vero. Se l'avessi recitato io non sarebbe stato più divertente

Dina Galli

EDIZIONI CORBACCIO - MILANO - LIRE DIECI
DOMANDATELO A TUTTI I LIBRAI

Chi vola vale
Chi non vola non vale
Chi vale e non vola è vile

N. 5081 - Corpo 12 (Scaramazzo) Kg. 2,65 (A-16, a-90)

Rappresentazioni Benefiche

123 Teatro Argentina 456

N. 5082 C.16 (Scaramuccia) Kg. 3,35 (A 12, a-50)

Nuestra Habitación

N. 1204 U. C.20 (Rimesso) Kg. 3,80 (A-8, a-38)

Studio Notarile

N. 1205 U. C.28 (Rimestare) Kg. 4,35 (A-7, a-24)

Protubérant

N. 1206 U. - Corpo 36 (Rimettere) Kg. 5,– (A-4, a-15)

Rimodernato

N. 1207 U. - Corpo 48 (Rimettitura) Kg. 5,70 (A-3, a-8)

Désolation

N. 1208 U. - Corpo 60 (Riminchionire) Kg. 7,50 (A-3, a-7)

Mastino

N. 5098 - Corpo 72 (Scaramucciare) Kg. 9,– (A-2, a-6)

Bombardati

N. 5099 - Corpo 84 (Scaraventare) Kg. 12.– (A-2, a 6)

Estaciónes

Tacca Italiana SERIE EBE, OMBREGGIATA *Classe* ***B***

N. 1538 U. - Corpo 16 (Richiudere) Kg. 2,40 (A-6, a-20)

La prosperité fait peu d'amis

N. 1539 U. - Corpo 20 (Ricignere) Kg. 2,75 (A-4, a-15)

Rigoletto Fedora Norma

N. 1540 U. - Corpo 28 (Ricino) Kg. 3,50 (A-4, a-10)

Mémorable Souvenir

N. 1541 U. - Corpo 36 (Ricisa) Kg. 4,25 (A-3, a-7)

Perfezionabile

Tacca Francese CARATTERI ALESSANDRO *Classe* ***B***

N. 1558 - Corpo 24-36 (Frammite) Kg. 4,75 (A-4, a-16)

Fabbrica Italiana Vetture

N. 1559 - Corpo 36-48 (Frana) Kg. 5,50 (A-3, a-12)

Concurso Tipográfico

N. 1560 - Corpo 44-56 (Franco) Kg. 7,– (A-3, a-8)

Japonesa

N.º 239.—Cuerpo 16.—1 Mín. 15 A 50 a.—Cerca 7,500 kilos, á Ptas. 7.

Ahora termina la fiesta de la Jota que ha re=

Asturias ZARAGOZA Córdoba

N.º 240.—Cuerpo 24.—1 Mín. 12 A 40 a.—Cerca 9 kilos, á Ptas. 6,50.

De las parejas de bailadores

Madrid SUIZA Bilbao

N.º 241.—Cuerpo 36.—1 Mín. 8 A 25 a.—Cerca 16,500 kilos, á Ptas. 6.

León MADRID Jaén

1 La Tempestad 2

N.º 242.—Cuerpo 48.—1 Mín. 4 A 16 a.—Cerca 18,500 kilos, á Ptas. 5,50.

Dr. Sala y Pons

N.º 243.—Cuerpo 60.—1 Mín. 4 A 12 a.—Cerca 22 kilos, á Ptas. 5.

3 Doloretes 5

ABCDEFGHIJKLM
NOPQRSTUVWX
12345 - YZ - 67890
abcdefghijklmnopqrst
Torino-uvwxyz-Social
GENOVA-CANTON

916. Corps 12. Min. ca. 6 kg

Allenstein Bunzlau Eisenach
Romanze Kinder des Südens Fragment
HEROS 3625 STERN

917. Corps 16. Min. ca. 8 kg

Hotel und Restaurant München
URACH 418 BRAUN

918. Corps 20. Min. ca. 10 kg

Berliner Schuh-Fabriken
ERICH KRAUSE

919. Corps 28. Min. ca. 12 kg

Alois Rademacher
THALHEIM

920. Corps 36. Min. ca. 16 kg

Actien-Gesellschaft Berolina
STARNBERG

921. Corps 36/48. Min. ca. 18 kg

Wiener Künstler-Bund
VIA AUSTRIA

922. Corps 48/60. Min. ca. 20 kg

Modernes Theater
FILIPPO

Cic. 12 - Classe B-l

Serie MONTEVIDEO

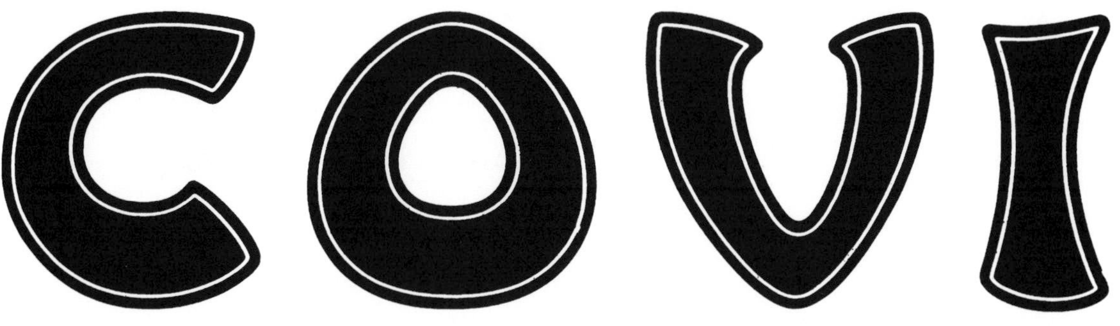

Cic. 18 - Classe C-g

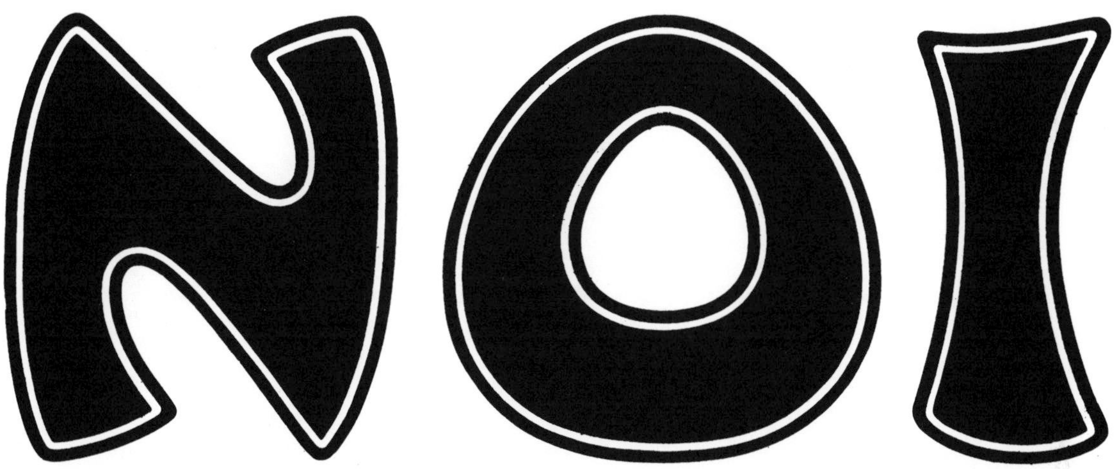

Cic. 20 - Classe C-n

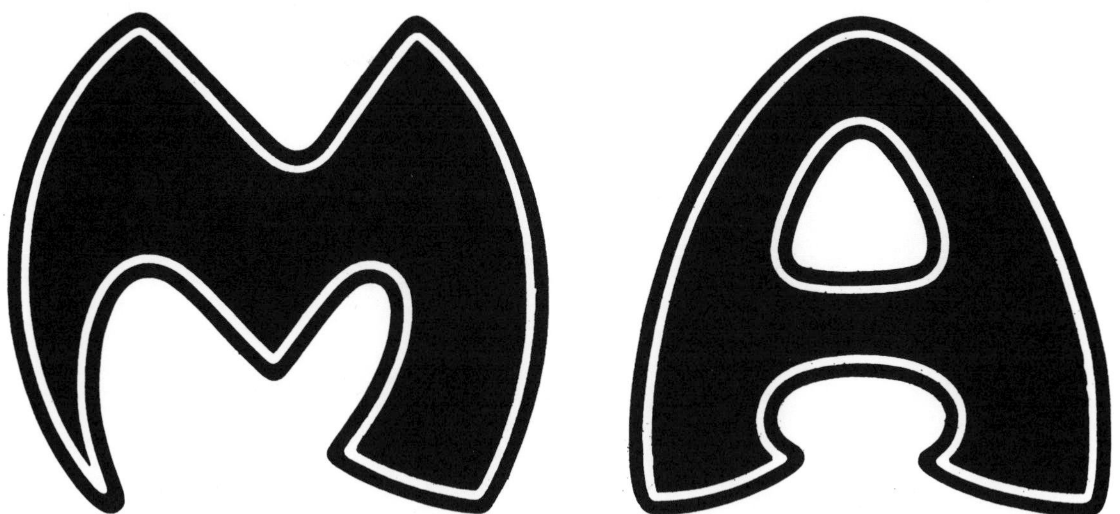

$5.50 48 POINT 6 A

CATCH 3

ONE ACE

REMOVED

$4.50 36 POINT 8 A

BICYCLIST

ROAD FINE

COST $289

PROSPECTUS, ANNONCES
& RÉCLAMES
COMPOSÉS AVEC NOS CARACTÈRES NOUVEAUX

Allainguillaume & Cie
21, RUE DU MONTPARNASSE

Gauthier

IMPRIMEUR-ÉDITEUR
3, Rue Malher
· ROUEN ·

Livres
Classiques
et de
Piété
Imagerie

BOBINO-HALL
Rue de la Gaîté
Tous les Soirs
*** CONCERT * PIÈCES

Produits des Colonies

FRUITS & PRIMEURS DE QUALITÉ EXTRA

Cafés, Thés, Chocolats

SPÉCIALITÉ DE RHUM DE LA MARTINIQUE

Robiquet & Langlais

38, RUE MONTMARTRE, 38

ARRIVAGES RÉGULIERS TOUS LES MARDI & SAMEDI

BISCUITS NONNETTES

Confiserie Gathinas

64, RUE DIDOT
5, PLACE BÉNARD
MAUBEUGE

AUX CAVES FRANÇAISES

Champagne — *Nos Vins de ce cru, sont universellement renommés*

Bordeaux — *Tous nos Vins du Médoc sont garantis de l'année 1890.*

RÉFÉRENCE DES CARACTÈRES EMPLOYÉS

Nos d'ord.	Désignation	Corps	Nos	Poids min.	Prix
11	Mauresques noires......	12	1139	2 k.	10 fr. le k°
12	Mexicaines blanches....	36	1164	8 k.	8 — —
13	Genre gothique (3 œils).	9	1070	2 k.	12 — —
14	Mexicaines blanches....	42	1165	9 k.	7,50 —
15	Antiques écrasées.......	6	757	1 k.	12 — —
16	Genre gothique (3 œils).	6	1069	1 k 50	14 fr. le k°
17	Antiques écrasées.......	5	1212	1 k.	14 — —
18	Arcadiennes..............	12	824	1 k 50	10 — —
19	Originales-Antiques......	6	755	1 k.	18 — —
20	Arméniennes allongées.	18	1178	3 k.	11 — —

Page **269 M**bis — 3000 ex.
5-1904

Caractères nouveaux nos 1164, 1165, 1166, 1196, 1197
DÉPOSÉS

ALLAINGUILLAUME & Cie
PARIS

LINING FACADE **SUPERIOR COPPER · POINT LINE · POINT SET · POINT BODY · MIXED TYPE** CONDENSED SERIES

Weights and Prices given are Approximate; see page 2. Cast on Uniform Line.

4 A 6 a | 60 Point Lining Facade Condensed | 6¾ lbs., **$4.70**

MINNESOTA MERCHANTS BANQUET

Real Estate Board 4 Elected Their President

4 A 6 a | 72 Point Lining Facade Condensed | 7 3/16 lbs., **$4.90**

SUPREME COURTS DECISION

Have Voted in Favor 3 of the Defense

3 A 5 a | 84 Point Lining Facade Condensed | 8¼ lbs., **$5.30**

PUBLISHERS AND STATIONERS

Pleasant Manner 6 Look Cheerful

THIRTY LINES RUNIC GROTESQUE ELONGATED

MOB

TWENTY LINES RUNIC GROTESQUE ELONGATED

DREGS

SUPERIOR COPPER MIXED TYPE
POINT LINE POINT SET POINT BODY

READ SHOES for Women $3.89

The Read shoe is making a great sensation among women and shoe dealers, on account of the stylish shapes, the fine workmanship, and remarkable leather from which they are made. Dealers have only to show the Shoe to sell them. The leather used in all Read Shoes is made by the United Leather Company whose name is a guarantee.

We are placing them with good shoe men everywhere, but if your dealer does not have them, we will be glad to send you a pair on receipt of $3.89, and will refund your money if not as represented. Our shoe book shows you over one hundred styles. Shall we send one?

Read Shoe Co.

Lastville

COMBINATION BORDER NO. 116

ELZEVIR COND. NO. 50

Weights and Prices given are Approximate; see page 2. Cast on Uniform Line.

6 A 10 a — 36 Point Elzevir Condensed No. 50 — $6\frac{13}{16}$ lbs., **$4.25**

HONESTY MAKES SOBRIETY
United States Great 84 War Department

6 A 9 a — 48 Point Elzevir Condensed No. 50 — $10\frac{7}{16}$ lbs., **$6.30**

GRAND SOCIAL EVENT
Crank Bachelors 8 Not Accepted

3 A 4 a — 60 Point Elzevir Condensed No. 50 — $7\frac{5}{8}$ lbs., **$4.60**

NORTHERN STEAMERS
United States 74 Leading Mine

3 A 4 a — 72 Point Elzevir Condensed No. 50 — $8\frac{1}{2}$ lbs., **$4.95**

SALEABLE GOODS
Many Styles 94 and Prices

Tacca Francese SERIE GROTTESCO LARGO NERO *Classe* **C**

N. **2349** - Corpo 6 (Natio) Kg. 1,25 (A-40)

GIOSUÈ CARDUCCI GIACOSA GIUSEPPE

N. **2350** - Corpo 6 (Natura) Kg. 1,50 (A-40)

MONTEVIDEO PEKINO STOKHOLM

N. **2351** - Corpo 8 (Natale) Kg. 2,– (A-30)

LA REPUBLIQUE FRANCAISE

N. **2352** - Corpo 10 (Nauta) Kg. 2,50 (A-24)

NULLA DIES SINE LINEA

N. **2353** - Corpo 12 (Navale) Kg. 3,– (A-24)

NAZIONALIZZANTE

N. **2354** - Corpo 14 (Nebbia) Kg. 3,50 (A-20)

BEATIFICAZIONE

N. **2355** - Corpo 18 (Nàvolo) Kg. 4,– (A-12)

CONOSCIUTO

N. **2356** - Corpo 24 (Naufragio) Kg. 5,– (A-8)

PRUDENTI

N. **2357** - Corpo 30 (Nave) Kg. 6,– (A-6)

CAXTON

N. **2358** - Corpo 36 (Navicello) Kg. 7,– (A-6)

SORTE

Tacca Italiana ITALICO NERO *Classe* **C**

N. 4724 U. - Corpo 20 (Sagola) Kg. 3,75 (A-40)

UNE MERVEILLEUSE ET BONNE CONDUITE

N. 4725 U. - Corpo 24 (Sagoma) Kg. 5,– (A-30)

MASINO STORIELLE ROMANE

N. 165 U. - Corpo 36 (Sagomare) Kg. 7,– (A-22)

SCORGE IL MAGNETO

N. 166 U. - Corpo 48 (Sagrestano) Kg. 9,25 (A-16)

BUONE PROSE

N. 4726 U. - Corpo 60 (Sagrestia) Kg. 10,– (A-12)

EXPOSITION

N. 4727 U. - Corpo 84 (Sagrinato) Kg. 11,– (A-12)

GENITURE

WASHINGTON SERIES

PATENTED

15

60 POINT 4 A 5 a $15 00

RICH Man

54 POINT 4 A 5 a $10 50

Dear GAME

48 POINT 4 A 5 a $10 00

FRIED Crabs

42 POINT 4 A 6 a $7 25

Best NEW Dish

36 POINT 5 A 8 a $6 75

TIN Pan

24 POINT 8 A 10 a $4 50

Daily RIDES

12 POINT 12 A 18 a $3 00

FISHERMAIDEN
Handsome Companion

8 POINT 18 A 24 a $2 50

ENCAMPMENT CUISINE
Palatable Dainties Served Gratis
1234567890

30 POINT 6 A 8 a $5 25

Flat RIMS

18 POINT 9 A 13 a $3 50

NOVEL Whalers

10 POINT 16 A 22 a $2 75

SAILING EXCURSION
Midnight Trip Advertised

6 POINT 22 A 32 a $2 25

DELIGHTFUL EVENING PASTIME
Repairing Fishing and Gunning Equipment
1234567890

NOVELTY SCRIPT

15

72 POINT 3 A 4 a $16 00

Rich Child

60 POINT 3 A 5 a $11 75

Love's Dream

48 POINT 3 A 6 a $9 00

Famous Battles

36 POINT 4 A 8 a $7 25

Lithographic Printing

24 POINT 5 A 12 a $5 25

Pay to the Order of Thomas Little
Sixteen Kicks with Heavy Boots

18 POINT 5 A 16 a $4 00

It Has Always Been Observed to be a Fact
"Truth Crushed to Earth Shall Rise Again"
1234567890

MARGRAF & FISCHER

MAINZ

WEIHERGARTEN 12

TEL. 5397

●

**AUTOTYPIEN
STRICHÄTZUNGEN
KOMBINIERTE
UND MEHRFARBEN-
ÄTZUNGEN**

EIN SCHUTZ-
ZEICHEN FÜR
SIE
ES BEDEUTET
VOLLENDUNG FÜR
DIE ERZEUGNISSE
DER FIRMA:
F. GUHL & CO.
GRAPHISCHE KUNSTANSTALT
UND KLISCHEEFABRIK
FRANKFURT · M

abcdefghijk

lmnopqrſst

uvwxyz

Ce caractère au pochoir est fait de matériel typographique et peut, comme aux exemples 1, 2, 3 être systématiquement élargi ou allongé

abc 1

abc 2

abcdefghik

achtung glas

3

abcdefghijk
lmnopqrſstu
vwxyz

Ce caractère est composé à l'aide de matériel typographique (lignes de laiton). La lettre a, ci dessous, montre comment les éléments sont assemblés.

aaaaaß a

graphische abteilung der
württembergischen
staatlichen
kunstgewerbeschule stuttgart

Par cet emploi on montre les transformations des formes de lettres (a, d, g, w).

DER EINDRINGLING
EIN JESUITENROMAN
VON
BLASCO IBAÑEZ
Berlin
Verlag von Emil Felber
1908

DEKORATIVE
KVNST
ZEITSCHRIFT
FVER
ANGEWANDTE
KVNST
N °2
I X.
JHRG:
F.H.EHMCKE
FHE
CLARA MOLLER-COBURG
HERAVSG: VON
HBRVCKMANN
VERL:
F. BRVCKMANN
ÄG: MVENCHEN
FHE

ABCDEFGHIJKL
MNOPQRSTUVW
abcdef . XYZ . ghijkl
mnopqrsſtuvwxyz
JOHANNESBURG
NATION . MICADO
Birmingham . Tunis
Hugo . Carmen . Plan
1234567890

Goldene Medaille

Haas Linien- und Kornraster

Dreifarbendruck-Raster = Universal-Drehraster

Goldene Medaille

Haas-Raster

anerkannt erstklassig

werden in der deutschen Reichsdruckerei, K.K.Österr., Kais. russischen Staatsdruckerei, im Kgl. bayr. topographischen Bureau des Kriegsministeriums sowie in allen großen Anstalten im In- und Ausland verwendet

Reparatur beschädigter Raster

Jede Größe und Linienweite sofort lieferbar

Fabrik und Lager:

Telephon-Anschluß No. 920

J. C. Haas, Frankfurt a. M. Zeisselstraße 11

Telegr.-Adr.: Aetzhaas Frankfurtmain

PLAKAT

Schriften und Zierat

in Blei und widerstandsfähigstem Hartholz in reichster Auswahl und jeder Grösse. Vignetten und Einfassungen wirksamster Art für Plakate. Bester Schutz der Holztypen gegen die Einwirkung von Feuchtigkeit durch Imprägnation

Paris 1900 Holzschriftenfabrik Grand Prix

J · G · Schelter & Giesecke · Leipzig

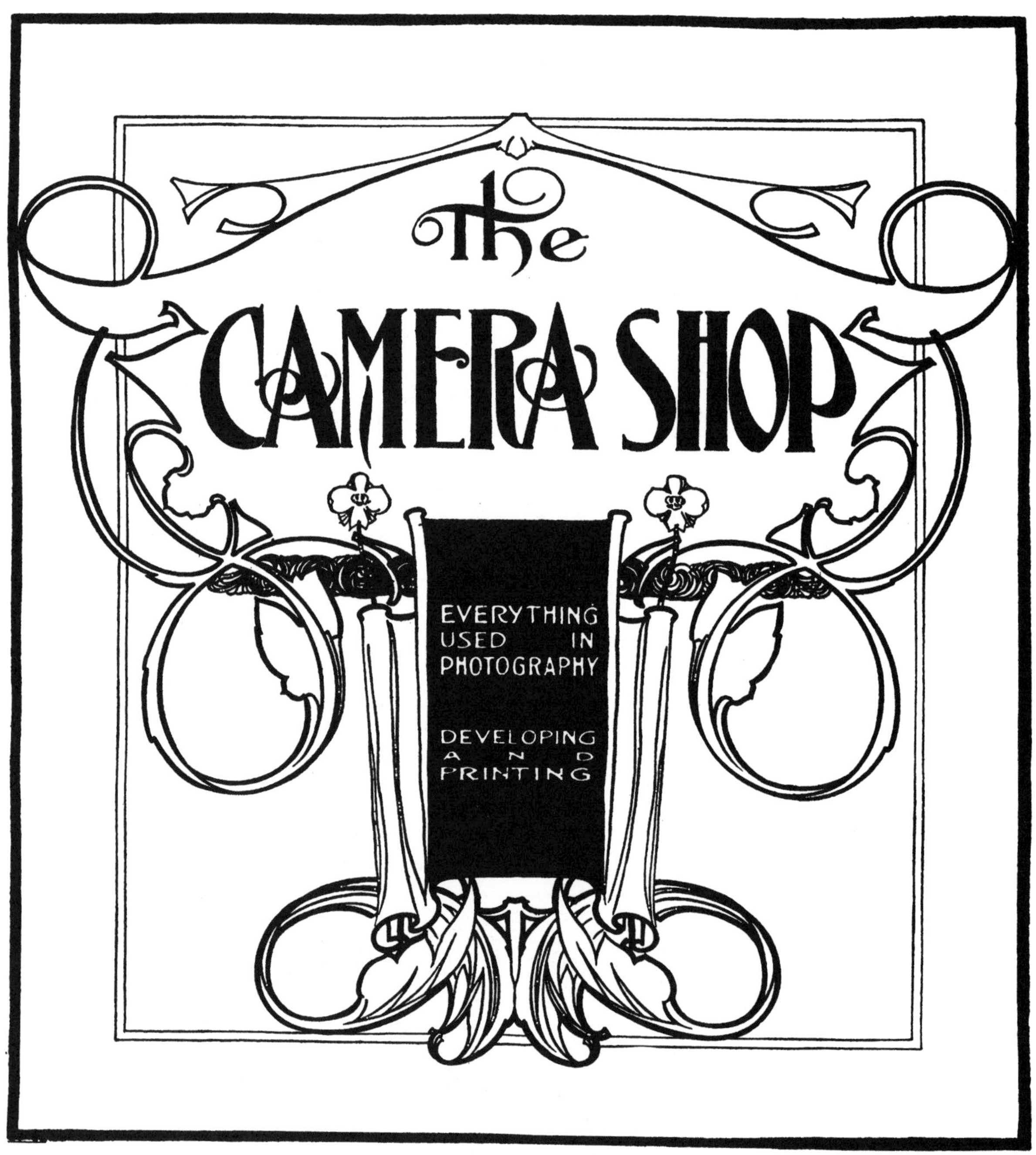
The
CAMERA SHOP
EVERYTHING USED IN PHOTOGRAPHY
DEVELOPING AND PRINTING

46
UP TO DATE
SIGNS
Abbott
AND
CO
CLASSIC
AND
ARTISTIC
MODERNISMS.
PHONE .SO.1058.

No. X5

Collection Stickers

Assorted Four Kinds to each 1000
Your own choice and selection

1000=$2.20

(No Quantity Prices)

No. X6

No. X1

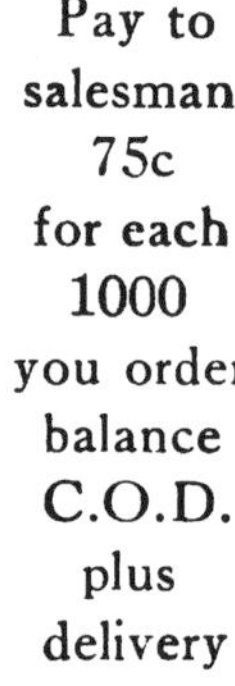
Pay to salesman 75c for each 1000 you order balance C.O.D. plus delivery charges

No. X2

No. X3

No. X4

Specify by number the stickers you desire

No. X7

No. X8

No. X9

Printed exactly as shown on gummed paper

No. X10

Collection Stickers

Assorted 4 kinds of 250 to each 1000 — your selection
Pay 75c Deposit Per 1000 — Balance C.O.D. Plus Delivery

$2.20 Per 1000

No. X67

No. X68

No. X69

No. X70

No. X71

No. X72

No. X73

No. X74

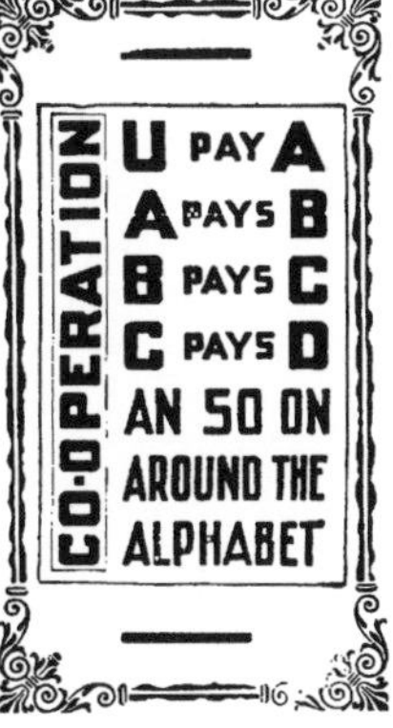

No. X75

and

Question Mark

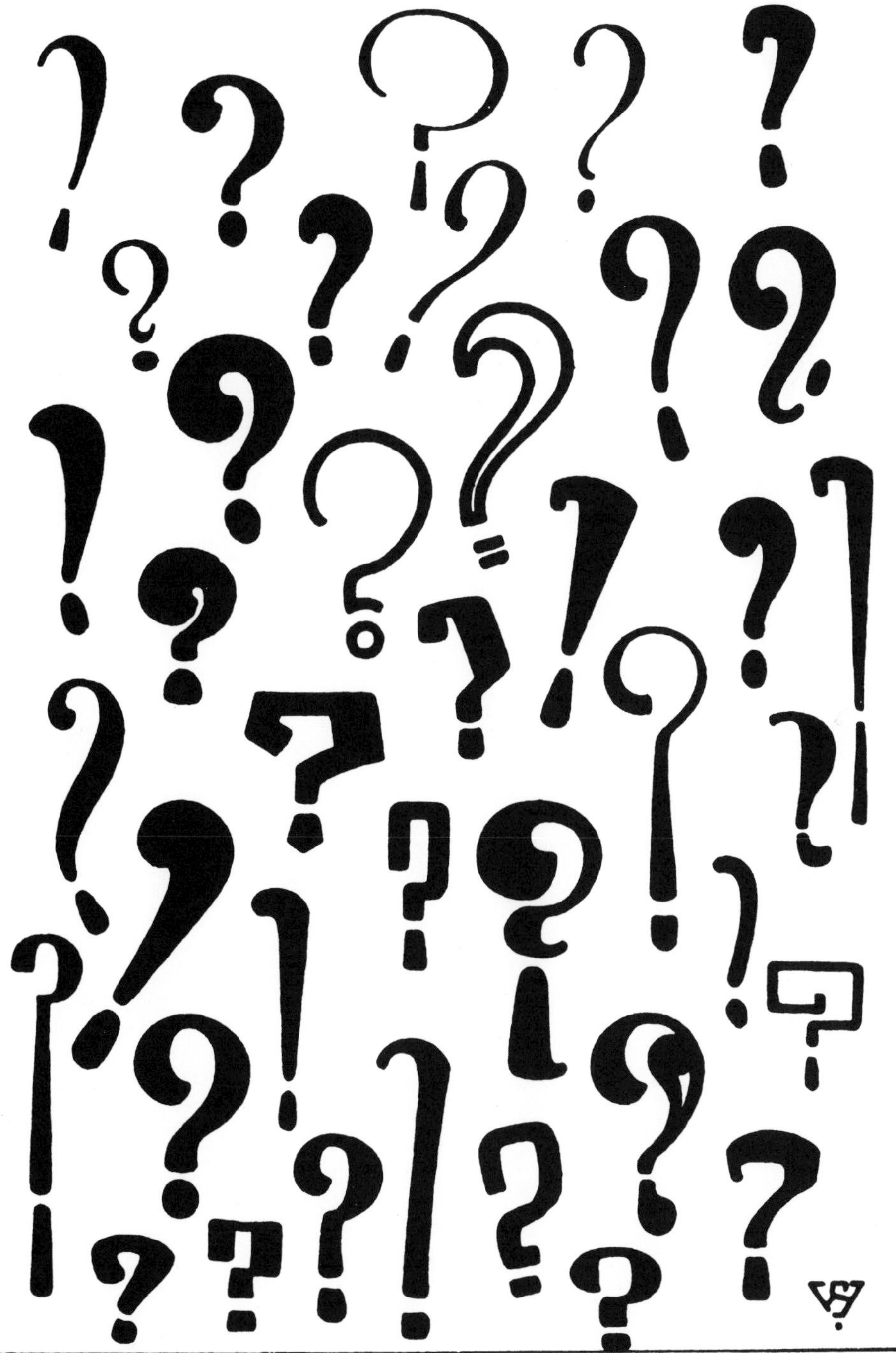

Red Beads 2

$11.00 60 Point 4 A 9 a

Sound 7 Chair

$10.00 54 Point 4 A 9 a

Correct Sizes 6

$9.00 48 Point 4 A 10 a

Human 8 Voices

$8.00 42 Point 4 A 10 a

German Branch 4

SIXTEEN LINES BASUTO CONDENSED INLINED

MEN

TWELVE LINES BASUTO CONDENSED INLINED

READ

EIGHT LINES BASUTO CONDENSED INLINED

POSTERS

SIX LINES BASUTO CONDENSED INLINED

AUGUST 23

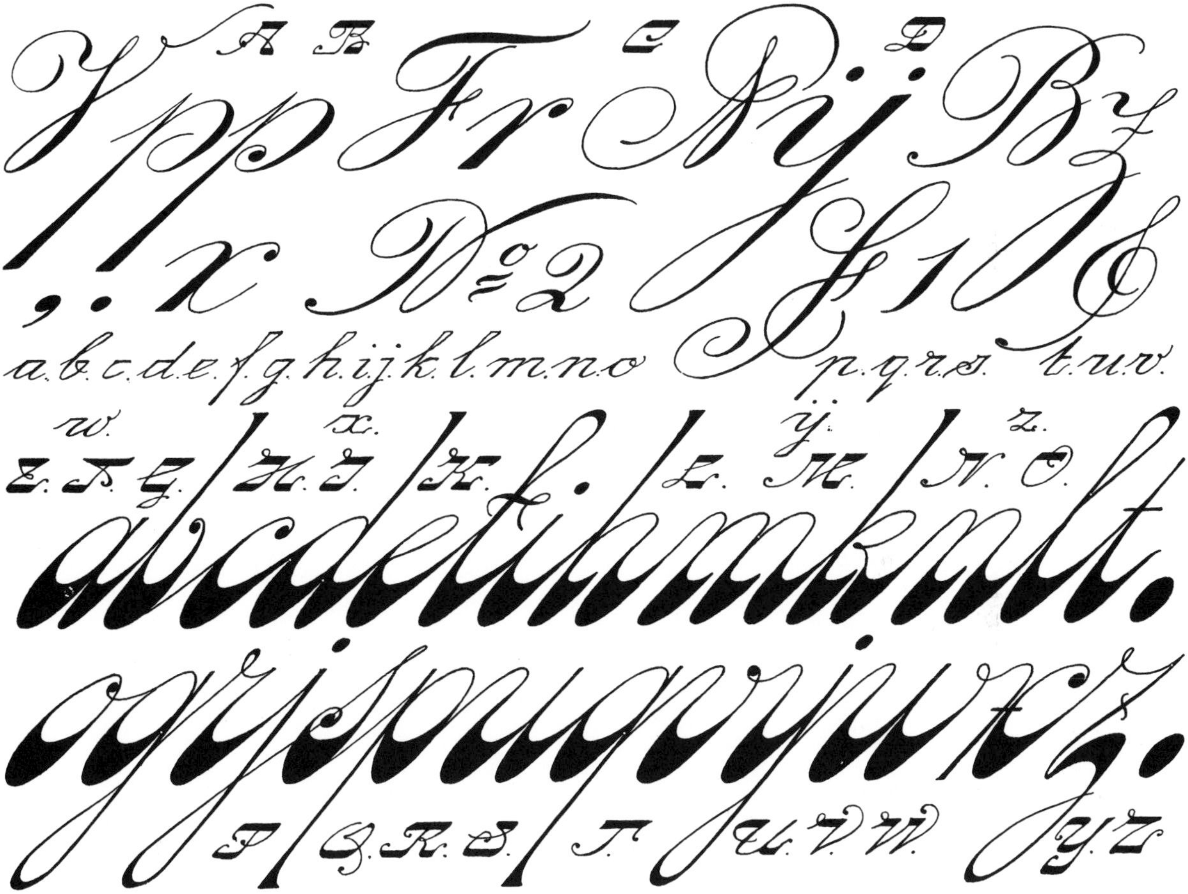

ABCDEFGHIJ
KLMNOPQRST
UVWXYZbdfht
lkaceimnnorsuvwz
gipxy & 1234567890.

ABCDEFGHIJ

KLMNNOPQJ

RSTUVWZYX

B · ARN · B

123467550

Asbach-Uralt-
Pralinen
CISSARZ

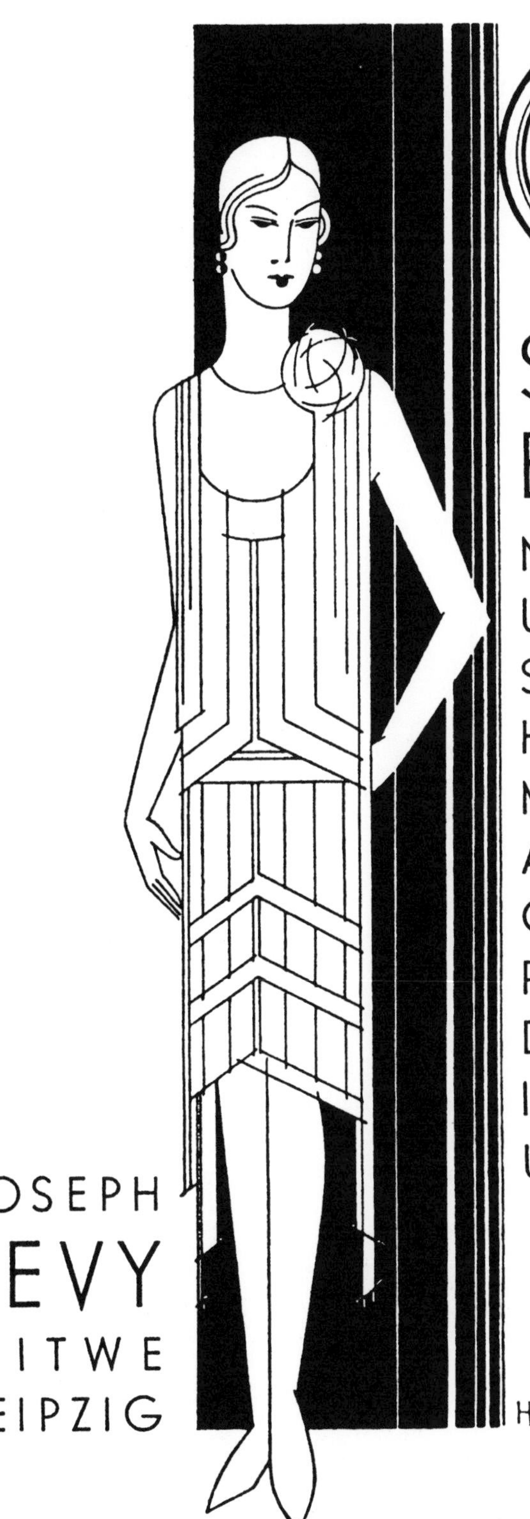
SAISON
ERÖFFNUNG
NACHMITTAGS-
U. ABEND-KLEIDER
SEITLICH ODER
HINTEN GERAFFT
MIT ODER OHNE
ATLAS-SCHLEPPE
GLOCKENRÖCKE
PRINZESSFORM
DER SCHLAGER
IN SCHWARZEM
U. WEISSEM TÜLL
JOSEPH
LEVY
WITWE
LEIPZIG
HANKE

TRANSITO

No. 2560 Corps 84/72 4 A, 7 a Minimum 21 Kg.

Bark

No. 2559 Corps 72/60 4 A, 10 a Minimum 16 Kg.

Canal
TOUR

No. 2558 Corps 60 5 A, 10 a Minimum 14 Kg.

Binder
STERK

No. 2557 Corps 48 5 A, 12 a Minimum 11 Kg.

Election
DESIRED

No. 2556 Corps 36 7 A, 17 a Minimum 10 Kg.

De Zetkast
MEUBELEN

No. 2555 Corps 28 9 A, 22 a Minimum 8 Kg.

Chance Natur
DEKORATION

No. 2554 Corps 24 12 A, 27 a Minimum 7 Kg.

Reise in Persien
Soll und Haben
FROHE STUNDEN

ABCDEFGHIJ
KLMNOPQR
STUVWXYZ
abcdefghijk
lmnopqrstu
vwxyz.,:;!?-)
1234567890

N.V. LETTERGIETERIJ „AMSTERDAM" VOORHEEN N. TETTERODE

Cic. 25 - Classe B-p

Serie TUNISI

Cic. 30 - Classe C-g

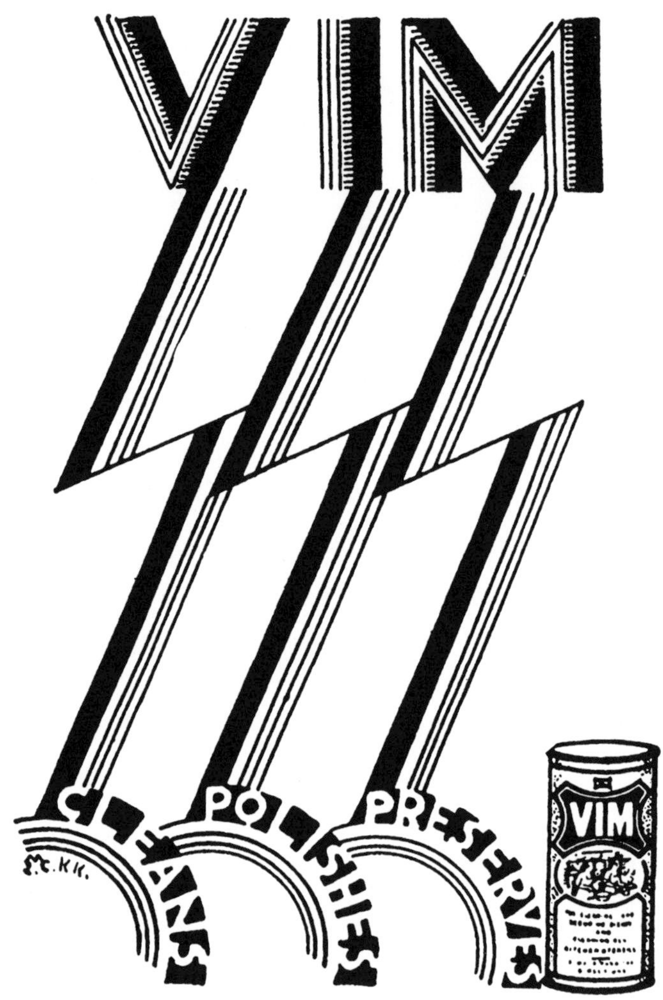

VIM

VIM—WOW !—IT'S WILD WHEN DIRT GETS IN ITS WAY IS VIM ★ VIM CLEANS POTS . PANS . CUTLERY . CROCKERY . BATHS AND SINKS . TILES AND PORCELAIN . GLAZED AND ENAMELLED SURFACES . FLOORS AND TABLES . DISHES . COOKING VESSELS . COOKING STOVES AND ALL KITCHEN UTENSILS : MAKES THEM LIKE NEW ★ VIM WHIZZES DIRT AWAY ★ LEVER BROTHERS LIMITED . PORT SUNLIGHT

SPEED • POWER • PICK-UP
EASE OF CONTROL • SAFETY
QUICK SHIFTING • ECONOMY

Chrysler "77" Royal Sedan, $1695 (Special Equipment Extra)

Performance only Chrysler gives!

Even the greatest of Chrysler's previous accomplishments—epochal as they have been—are completely overshadowed by the new Multi-Range Chryslers. In them, power, speed, acceleration, economy and safety are raised to the highest degree. New and larger engines, down-draft fuelization, and the exclusive Multi-Range transmission and gear shift create performance never before even closely approached.

And there's new beauty in these marvelous cars—new comfort, too, in their larger, roomier, exquisitely upholstered bodies, with fitments by Cartier, the famous international jeweler.

As pacemakers of performance and criterions of style, the new Multi-Range Chryslers transcend even Chrysler's previous best so decisively that they leave no basis for comparison.

FEATURES:—Larger, more powerful engines . . . 7-bearing counter-balanced crankshaft . . . multi-range four-speed transmission and gear shift . . . down-draft carburetion . . . Chrysler weatherproof four-wheel hydraulic brakes . . . paraflex springs . . . rubber spring shackles . . . hydraulic shock absorbers . . . oversize 6-ply balloon tires . . . roomier bodies of dreadnought construction . . . metalware by Cartier et Cie.

• • •

All Chrysler models will be exhibited at the National Automobile Shows. In addition, special displays during the New York Show, January 4th to 11th, in the Commodore Hotel and during the Chicago Show, January 25th to February 1st, in the Balloon Room and lobbies of the Congress Hotel.

MULTI-RANGE
CHRYSLER

From $2895 to $3475 **77** From $1595 to $1795 **70** From $1295 to $1525 **66** From $985 to $1065 — ALL PRICES F.O.B. DETROIT

CLEVER MAKE-UP

NINE-TENTHT OF BEAUTY

Beauty and make-up experts the world over agree that Beauty is nine-tenths Clever Make-up. Connoisseurs of True Beauty every-where admit it to be a fact. Why?

Probably only one stage and screen star in a hundred is naturally beautiful. But on the stage and screen, all actresses look beautiful. What is their secret? Clever make-up! And what is Clever Make-up? First, using natural cosmetics that give only the true bloom of youth that nature intended. Second, knowing how to apply these cosmetics to give the illusion of a perfectly proportioned face.

Too much has already been said about natural beauty. Deep down in her heart every woman knows how beautiful she really is. What she wants to know is how much more beautiful she can appear to be. Clever Make-up is the key that opens the gates of New Beauty - and it can really be achieved in such a few minutes! By following the simple suggestions given in our booklet you can make yourself appear more beautiful than you ever before dreamed possible.

KISSPROOF

PARIS CHICAGO·LONDON

BRISTOL

No. 2490 Corps 60 — 7 A — Minimum 16 Kg.

LETTERS

No. 2489 Corps 48 — 7 A — Minimum 12 Kg.

CONSIDER

No. 2488 Corps 36 — 11 A — Minimum 9 Kg.

HUSMODERNS

No. 2487 Corps 28 — 12 A — Minimum 7 Kg.

BRUXELLES NICE

No. 2486 Corps 24 — 15 A — Minimum 6 Kg.

ROTATIE MACHINES

No. 2485a Corps 20 — 19 A — Minimum 5 Kg.

BARNEPIGE

No. 2485 Corps 16 — 23 A — Minimum 4 Kg.

MOOIE LETTER

No. 2484 Corps 12 — 29 A — Minimum 3 Kg.

BOEKVERSIERING

A B C D E F G H I J
K L M N O P Q R S
T U V W X Y Z &
. , ; : ' ! ? -)
1 2 3 4 5 6 7 8 9 0

Bovenstaande figuren worden bij ieder corps bijgeleverd
Les ornements ci-dessus sont livrés dans chaque corps

N.V. LETTERGIETERIJ „AMSTERDAM" VOORHEEN N. TETTERODE

The LETTER
has a color Value!

CORSAGE

When drawing letters watch your styles, do not mix or errors result!

CORSAGE

A letter — may be altered to ones need-for correct spacing

The thin B E F I J L P R S T V

medium A D H K U X Y Z

oval C G Q *wide* M N W

This does not apply to all alphabets

LETTER THAT EXPRESSES GRACE AND STYLE, IN OTHER WORDS THE "CHIC" SO TYPICAL OF THE FRENCH PEOPLE. ~ ~ ~

IT IS NOT A LETTER FOR BOLD DISPLAY BUT ONE THAT CREATES THE ATMOSPHERE OF REFINEMENT. ~

FRENCH LETTER FORMS BRING US A UNIQUE QUALITY OF TONE THAT IS TRULY DISTINCTIVE. ~

Werkstätten für Buch- und Steindruck.
Rudolf Kleinhempel.
Telephon Nr. 4865. Dresden A. Fürsten-strasse 97.

ILLUSTRIERTE HALB-MONATSCHRIFT FÜR ARCHITEKTUR & KUNST-GEWERBE
ORGAN DES BUNDES DEUTSCHER ARCHITEKTEN (B.D.A.) UND VERÖFFENTLICHUNGSORGAN DES DEUTSCHEN WERKBUNDES (D.W.B.)

KUNST GEWERBE BLATT

HEFT 7

APRIL 1912

BAND XXIII

REDAKT: FRITZ HELLWAG IN BERLIN-ZEHLENDORF. VERLAG VON E.A. SEEMANN IN LEIPZIG

NIEDERRHEINISCHE
ELEKTRIZITÄTS
GESELLSCHAFT
BERGS &
WILDERMUTH
KREFELD.

WIRZ &
SCHLÖSSER
G.M. KÖLN B.H.
COLUMBASTRASSE. 6
FERNSPR. 384 GEGR. 1840

MONTHLY ELECTRIC REVIEW

18 Point
10 A — $1.90

A CRAFT PAPER DEVOTED TO ALL THE USES OF ELECTRICAL APPARATUS, USEFUL TO ELECTRICIANS OR JOBBERS, SPECIALLY ARRANGED ARTICLES BY BEST AUTHORITY, REPORTS, NOTES

24 Point
8 A — $2.35

PRICE, YEAR, $4.50
SAMPLE BY MAIL

ABCDEFGHIJKL

MNOPQRSTUVW

XYZ·123456789

ABCDEFGHJ

IKLMNOPQ

RSTUVWXYZ

ABCDEFGHIJKLMN

OPQRSTUVWXYZ

MIG
1903

MODERNE ANZEIGEN

die das Auge des Zeitungslesers fesseln sollen, müssen mit kraftvollen, schönen Schriften gesetzt werden. Unsere Herold wird an jeder Stelle ihre Schuldigkeit tun, denn sie ragt durch künstlerische Eigenart, Kraft und Schönheit hervor. Außerdem hat sie technische Vorzüge. Sie ist derb und dauerhaft. Das störende Fleisch unter der Linie ist durch zweckmäßige Form der Unterlängen so weit wie möglich fortgefallen. Dies ist sehr wesentlich bei Inseratsatz, wo jeder Millimeter Raum bares Geld bedeutet und deshalb voll ausgenutzt, also mit Schrift gefüllt werden muß

H. BERTHOLD AKT.-GES., BERLIN SW 29

Jede Hausfrau, die ihre Wäsche schonen will, und der es darauf ankommt, die Wäsche blendend weiß zu waschen, ohne ätzende Stoffe anzuwenden, nehme zum Waschen nur das Seifenpulver von Dr. Richard Neuberg.

Natolin

Dieses Seifenpulver ist so vorzüglich, daß es genügt, die Wäsche einmal damit einzuweichen, um sie dann mit Leichtigkeit, ohne sie erst lange mit schädlicher Seife kochen zu müssen, blendend weiß waschen zu können. Das Seifenpulver Natolin ist schon vielen Hausfrauen unentbehrlich geworden, denn es spart Zeit, Feuerung, und schont die Wäsche. Erhältlich in Seifenläden

HALB UND HALB

auch Himmelstau genannt, ist ein sehr bekömmlicher Likör, zugleich ein die Verdauung stark förderndes Mittel. Halb und Halb stärkt den Magen und wirkt besser als Medizin. Man achte beim Einkauf genau auf die Schutzmarke RS, sowie auf den Namenszug des Erfinders Heinrich Brodeck. Zu haben in allen Delikateß-Geschäften

Möbelfabrik Hans Winterfeld & Co.

Potsdamerstraße 156, liefert moderne Wohnungs-Einrichtungen in einfachster bis feinster Ausstattung billig. Polstersachen und Teppiche, Gardinen und Stores sind in großer Auswahl am Lager. Man verlange den neuesten Katalog, welcher franko versandt wird

Frisier-Schule Marietta Heinemann, geprüfte Lehrerin, Rheingasse 3, lehrt in kurzer Zeit alle Mode-Frisuren

Wo kauft man sehr billig die besten Cigarren?

Direkt bei der Fabrik, denn von dort können sie billiger geliefert werden, als von einem Privatgeschäft. Wir geben an jedermann hochfeine Qualitäten unserer Cigarren zum Engrospreise ab. Händler erhalten keinen Rabatt. Man verlange die Preisliste. Unsere Cigarren genießen durch ihre Feinheit und die Vorzüglichkeit in Aroma und Geschmack einen Weltruf. Alle Fabrikate, welche zum Verkauf gelangen, sind bereits gut abgelagert. Bestellungen von mindestens 200 Stück erfolgen postfrei

Gebrüder Neuheim, Hamburg

SCHMÜCKE DEIN HEIM

Freunde der Kunst bitte ich, meine neue Ausstellung von Ölgemälden Aquarellen, Pastellen, Radirungen und Stahl-Stichen zu besichtigen. Kunst-Handlung E. HEMER, Berlin

Wer einen eleganten Stiefel liebt, der auch bequem ist und wie ein Maßstiefel sitzt, kaufe jetzt nur noch Heinrich Neubauers

Patent-Stiefel

Dieser Stiefel ist für jeden Fuß genau passend vorrätig und übertrifft durch chike Form, hochfeines Aussehen alle anderen Fabrikate, er ist ein vollkommener Ersatz für jeden nach Maß angefertigten Stiefel. Neubauers Patent-Stiefel ist für Damen, Herren und Kinder in allen größeren Schuh-Geschäften und bei Heinrich Neubauer, Berlin W, Lützowstraße 43, zu haben

Heimburg in Thüringen

ein herrlicher Sommer-Aufenthalt für jeden Städter. In schöner Lage, mitten im Walde gelegen, bietet Heimburg alle Vorzüge eines guten, gesunden Erholungs-Ortes. Auch den weniger bemittelten Reisenden wird hier in soliden Pensionen bei freundlichen Familien Gelegenheit gegeben, sich ohne bedeutenden Kostenaufwand den Aufenthalt in der Sommerfrische zu gönnen. Aber auch für die verwöhntesten Reisenden ist durch vornehme Hotels, die mit allem Komfort der Neuzeit ausgestattet sind, vortrefflich gesorgt. Moderne Luft-, Licht- und Sonnenbäder stehen den Sommergästen zur Verfügung. An besonders schönen Tagen werden Wagenfahrten in die Umgegend unternommen, an denen sich jeder beteiligen kann. Morgens pünktlich 7 Uhr versammeln sich sämtliche Teilnehmer im Kurhause, wo die Wagen halten. Von hier aus geht die Fahrt durch den herrlichen Thüringer Wald, an idillischen Seen vorbei, nach dem Restaurant „Waldfrieden“, wo gefrühstückt wird. Nachdem begiebt sich die Gesellschaft in den Wald und unterhält sich durch fröhliche, gemeinschaftliche Spiele und Spaziergänge. Um 11 Uhr wird die Rückfahrt angetreten. Der Aufenthalt in Heimburg wird demnach Niemand gereuen, denn, wie man aus dieser Beschreibung sieht, ist es für jeden Erholung Suchenden ein gesunder, famoser

Luftkurort

RUHL

Dieser Raum ist frei für beliebigen Schriftsatz

Die grosse dekorative Wirkung von Titelzeilen wie die hier abgedruckten, wird besonders für Umschläge und feine Plakate auszunutzen sein. Schrägstriche können ohne Schwierigkeit aus Bahnenlinien geschnitten, ev. durch eine Kombination passender Bogenstücke ersetzt werden.

Unsere Linien-Elemente erhalten sich lange gut und brauchbar, einige Sorge lege man nur auf zweckmäßige Behandlung der scharfen Ecken. Nimmt man die Stereotypie zu Hilfe, so schont man das Material und nutzt es dabei am besten aus.

Grosslinige Monogramme und ähnliche Buchstaben-Verbindungen einfacher Art wie HB lassen sich aus diesen Linien-Elementen sehr leicht bilden.

Ein grosser Vortheil der Elemente ist, dass man die freien Räume innerhalb der Figuren überall mit Schrift ausfüllen kann. Bei Inseratsatz ist dies von Wichtigkeit, weil der oft theuer bezahlte Raum gut ausgenützt wird.

HB

Versuchen Sie einmal Hardinger Sprudel!

Bestes natürliches Mineralwasser, erfrischend, durststillend, säuretilgend und die Verdauung befördernd. In Gebinden 30 Fl. 3 Mark. G. BREUER, HARDINGEN.

Stellengesuche

Ein eigen Heim

sollte das Ziel jedes sorgsamen Familienvaters sein, umsomehr als dies Ziel beinahe ohne jede Kapital-Anlage, sowie ohne größeren Aufwand als die gewöhnliche Jahresmiethe zu erreichen ist. Im südlichen Theile des Stadtwaldes hat die Gesellschaft „**Sanitas**" Terrain erworben, auf dem verschieden grosse Wohnhäuser im Villen-Stil nebst Nebengebäuden und Garten errichtet werden sollen. Auskunft erteilt „**Sanitas**" A.-G., Charlottenburg.

Tinte!

Für Schnellschrift haben wir eine neue Tinte zusammengestellt, welche an Leichtflüssigkeit und schöner Färbung Alles übertrifft.

Diese Universal-Tinte

ist noch eine Stunde nach dem Trocknen copirfähig, sie kann also als Buch- und Copirtinte benutzt werden. Preis 1 l M. 3.

A. Rossmann, Berlin.

Bad Ems

Hotel Schultze

Vornehmstes Etablissement am Orte. Begünstigt durch ruhige, geschützte Lage am Walde. Brunnen, Kur- und Badeanstalten in der Nähe. Angenehmes Wohnen, auch in der heissesten Jahreszeit. Von den Herren Aerzten zu gleichzeitigem Luftkur- und Badeaufenthalt empfohlen. Prächtiger Garten mit sechs Spielplätzen und Pavillons. Eleganter Speisesaal, Lesesalon, Rauchzimmer. Zivile Logis- und Pensionspreise. Hausdiener am Bahnhof.

Prospekte auf Wunsch kostenlos

Abonnements-Einladung

Wir machen unsere werten Leser darauf aufmerksam, daß am 1. Oktober unser 4. Quartal beginnt und der Residenz-Bote schon jetzt mehr als 40000 Abonnenten besitzt. Die Redaktion des

Residenz-Boten

für Potsdam und umliegende Ortschaften wird stets bestrebt sein, ihre Leser in politischer, wirtschaftlicher und wissenschaftlicher Beziehung aufs beste zu unterrichten. Außerdem bringt der Residenz-Bote täglich eine Unterhaltungsbeilage mit den neuesten Romanen und Novellen von ersten Autoren.

Der Residenz-Bote erscheint täglich und kostet vierteljährlich frei ins Haus M. 2.80. Post-Zeitungsliste 839

Gute Bücher bilden für jede Familie eine Fundgrube von Belehrung und Anregung. In allen Volkskreisen macht sich das Bedürfnis nach guter und preiswerter Lektüre bemerkbar. Bestellen Sie den prachtvoll illustrierten Novitätenkatalog von

Ernst Reutters Buchverlag, Leipzig

Sie sparen viel

Geld

wenn Sie unsere Linien-Elemente erwerben. Mit den Serien 28—33 läßt sich eine große Zahl sehr wirkungsvoller Inserat-Figuren leicht herstellen.

Herkules-Initialen

1156. Corps 60/66. 1 Satz, bestehend aus den nachstehend abgedruckten 14 Figuren (je 2 Stück) M. 30.—
Einzelpreise: die nicht geklinkten Figuren B C D E G S à M. 1.—, die übrigen à M. 1.50

A B C D E H
F K M L T
G R S

1157. Corps 72/84.
14 Figuren wie oben abgedruckt.
1 Satz à 2 Stück M. 35.-

Einzelpreise: die nicht geklinkten Figuren B C D E G S à M. 1.25 die übrigen à M. 1.75

A K T

1158. Corps 84/96.
14 Figuren wie oben abgedruckt
1 Satz à 2 Stück M. 40.—

Einzelpreise: die nicht geklinkten Figuren B C D E G S à M. 1.50 die übrigen à M. 2.25

D R M

Die vorliegenden, bei richtiger Anwendung ausserordentlich wirksamen Initialen zur

Herkules

werden zum Teil mehrfach ausgeklinkt geliefert, um die Anbringung des Textes bis dicht an die Figur zu ermöglichen. Jede Grösse der Initialen passt für verschiedene Grade der Herkules.

Auch an dieser Stelle geklinkt, für Notizen.

Anzeigen und Inserate werden vom Leser nur dann beachtet, wenn diese durch wirkungsvolle Arrangements das Auge auf den ersten Blick festzuhalten vermögen. Wir pflegen schon seit Jahren die Ausstattung von Inseraten und die neuzeitliche Reklame in ihren verschiedenen Formen, sodaß wir in der Lage sind, Ihnen mit Mustern und Vorschlägen zur Hand zu gehen. Wir bitten unsere Prospekte zu verlangen.
Reklame-Institut „HAMMONIA" Hamburg, Jungfernstieg 8

Die Herkules-Initialen sind zwar zum Gebrauch mit der Herkules bestimmt, können aber auch mit anderen Schriften und, wie dieses Beispiel zeigt, besonders mit der Carola gebraucht werden, weil diese denselben Duktus einer Pinselschrift aufweist.

Reklame

Für Zeitungs-Druckereien ist die Gelegenheit gegeben, in der einfachsten Art ganz besonders wirkungsvolle Inseratsätze zu schaffen. Die Anschaffung der Reklameschriften Herkules und Carola, sowie der hier gezeigten Initialen als Material für Inseratsatz

Bitte zu beachten!

bezahlt sich!

Schriftgießerei

Messinglinien-Fabrik, Stereotypie und Galvanoplastik
Einfassungen, Schriften und Vignetten in allen Geschmacksrichtungen
Buchdruckerei-Einrichtungen in jeder Größe in kürzester Zeit lieferbar

Musterbücher stehen auf Wunsch unberechnet sowie franko zu Diensten

Julius Klinkhardt, Leipzig

Farbenfabrik Otto Baer, Radebeul-Dresden

Schwarze Schnelltrockenfarbe "VORAN"

Vorzüge: Trocknet auf rauhen, weichen und Kunstdruckpapieren von Bogen zu Bogen. — Auf holzfreien Druck- und mittelfesten Medianpapieren in zirka 10 Min. Auf Ullstein'schen Umschlagpapieren in zirka 15 Min. Auf Bücherstoff- und Hartpostpapieren in zirka 20 Min. Auf Elfenbeinkarton in zirka 25 Minuten **selbst bei größten Klischee- und Schriftflächen.**

"Voran" enthält kein Sikkativ.
"Voran" greift die Walzen nicht an.
"Voran" trocknet auf den Walzen nicht fest.
"Voran" eignet sich für Autotypie-, Illustrations- und Akzidenzdruck.

"Voran" kostet in

Qual.	0	I	II	III	
Mark	6,—	5,—	4,—	3,—	per Kilo

Versuchen Sie diese Farbe, Sie werden erstaunt sein von diesem großen Fortschritt!

Fabrik schwarzer und bunter Buch- und Steindruck-Farben

Lichtdruckfarben o Blechdruckfarben o Firnis-Siederei und Rußbrennerei o Walzenmasse "The Best"

Vertretung und Lager für Berlin:
Oscar Hartmann, Südende-Berlin, Hermannstraße 4
Fernsprecher Amt Tempelhof No. 3037

Für Österreich-Ungarn: **J. Zucker, Wien II/1, Taborstr. 52a**

Plakat-Schriften

Beste und billigste Bezugsquelle

Franz Gerhardt & Rudolph, Leipzig-Gohlis

Verlangen Sie Muster! Nur erstklassige Fabrikate

Mit lebhaftem Interesse durchblättert jeder Fachmann die Musterhefte der

Ideal-Schreibschrift

sowie der ***Ridingerschrift*** *von*

Benjamin Krebs Nachfolger, Frankfurt a. M.

F. M. Weiler's

Liberty Machine Works

BERLIN W

Kronen-Strasse 8

Liberty-Maschinen Grosse Auswahl in der seit **45 Jahren** bewährten Bauart

1859—1904

Von allen Tiegeldruck-Maschinen ist die **Liberty** die bekannteste, die **einfachste**, die **stärkste**, die **leistungsfähigste**, die **praktischste**. Deshalb ist sie in allen Ländern der Welt, wo Buchdruckereien sind, erfolgreich eingeführt worden

752. Corps 72. Min. ca. 20 kg

Gerhart Heidner

Jungbrunnen

753. Corps 84. Min. ca. 25 kg

Bunte Woche

Andalusien

753a. Corps 96. Min. ca. 30 kg

Niederbronn

Kulmbach

Kaufhaus=Fraktur

Reisender junge tüchtige Verkaufskraft, repräs. Erscheinung, Fachmann der Eisenbranche, mit dem Betriebe der Eisengießerei und der Messingröhren=Fabrikation in jeder Hinsicht vertraut, sucht Stellung in großer **Eisengießerei** Gefl. Angeb. unter B. 25 an d. Exped. d. Bl.

Touristen-Vereinigung wünscht noch gesellige Herren als Mitglieder aufzunehmen. Versammlung jeden Mittwoch 9 Uhr im Deutschen Wirtshaus.

Bade=Anstalt des Westens

Martin Luther=Straße 52. Modern eingerichtete Bade=Anstalt für Herren und Damen, mit großem Schwimmbassin. Wannen= und medizinische Bäder genau nach Vorschrift unter Aufsicht geprüfter Wärter. Massagen und Packungen streng gewissenhaft.

Jongleur der 17 Bälle und 9 Keulen perfekt jongliert, Parterre springt, einarmig Handstand auf dem Schlappseil macht und Schnellmaler ist, auch als Kunstradfahrer auftritt, sucht Engagement bei erstklassiger Spezialitäten=Bühne. Angebote erbeten an Karl Tietzmann, München, Regensburgerstraße 43

Erholung findet man am besten im Orte Neuhagen an der Elbe. Gute Pensionen sind billig bei freundlichen Landleuten zu haben und ist auch für die Unterhaltung der Sommergäste in jeder Weise gesorgt. Der Ort ist schön gelegen und hat viel **Wald**

Lager-Verwalter der Papier=Branche, gelernter Buchbinder, gesetzten Alters, in jeder Beziehung erfahren und geübter Papierkenner, mit der Führung der Lagerbücher durchaus vertraut und befähigt, dem Personal energisch vorzustehen, sucht entsprechende Stellung. Gefl. Offerten unter „Albert 41" an die Geschäftsstelle d. Bl. erb.

Tüchtiger Buchhalter in einfacher und doppelter Buchführung, Korrespondenz perfekt, sucht Stellung. Gefl. Offerten unter S. 326 an die Exped. d. Bl.

Junges Mädchen mit guter Handschrift, für Expedition sofort gesucht. Bewerberinnen wollen sich schriftlich melden bei Heinrich Kuhnert, Bärwaldstraße 246.

Sie haben Erfolg in jeder Beziehung sicher und schnell!

Verlangen Sie unser Werk: „Willenskraft des Menschen", von Professor Hartmann. Das Buch gibt u. a. Anleitung, wie man sich um eine Stellung bewirbt, wie man als Schriftsteller einen Ruf erlangt, wie man höher gestellten Personen, Vorgesetzten rc. imponiert, wie man als Kaufmann gute Geschäfte macht usw. In gutverständlicher Sprache geschrieben, ist das Werk für jedermann ein sehr wertvoller Schatz. Preis 4.50 Mark. **Verlag Merkur, Potsdam**

Verkäuferin Junges Mädchen mit guten Zeugnissen, in großem Konfektionshause tätig, sucht andere Stellung. Off. V. 3, Exped. d. Bl.

Platz=Vertreter von leistungsfähiger großer Seifen=Fabrik für Berlin und Vororte sofort gesucht. Bew. muß repräsentieren können und gewandt im Verkehr mit der Kundschaft sein. Der Posten ist gutsaläriert und sichert eine angenehme und dauernde Stellung. Nur Herren, die bereits mit Erfolg gereist haben und Branche=Kenntnisse besitzen, wollen ihre Angebote unter P. V. 86 an die Geschäftsstelle d. Bl. richten.

Hotel Koburg

Elegantes, im modernen Stile eingerichtetes Hotel. Englische und französische Küche. Weine in= und ausländischer Firmen **Besitzer Rudolf Beckert**

Persianer sowie andere kostbare echte Pelze, Bisam u. Skunks in besonders prächtigen Stücken für die Hälfte ihres sonstigen Wertes. Pelze=Engroshaus Stern, Berlin

Ein nützliches Ding für jede Wirtschaft

ist die neue Waschmaschine Ideal. Größte Sauberkeit der Wäsche bei schonender Behandlung. Zu jeder Zeit Vorführung der Maschine im Verkaufslokal Knesebeck=Straße 16

Reklame-Zeichner wirklich tüchtige u. künstlerisch durchgebildete Kraft für große Reklame=Arbeiten sucht **Warenhaus Erich Heinbeck**

Vertretung für Köln und Vororte von erster ausländischer Motoren-Fabrik per sofort zu vergeben Angebote unter F 12 an d. Exp.

Farben! Prima Aquarell= und Oelfarben, sowie alle Mal= und Zeichenutensilien bester Qualität. Hermann Bern, Leipzig

Pensions-Anstalt für junge Mädchen aus guter Familie. Gewissenhafte Ausbildung im Kochen und allen anderen wirtschaftlichen Arbeiten durch bewährte Lehrerinnen. Alles Nähere durch die Vorsteherin Frau **Marta Krüger, Bergstr. 28**

Wohnungen mit Balkon, drei u. vier Zimmer in neuem Haus. Akazienstraße 29

Schönheit und ewige Jugend wird jeder Dame durch täglichen Gebrauch von Marburgs antiseptischer Lilienmilch=Seife Venus erhalten bleiben. Diese Seife verleiht der Haut ein zartes jugendfrisches Aussehen, beseitigt Mitesser, Pickel, Flechten und Sommersprossen usw. in kurzer Zeit. Für Kinder ist die Seife auch sehr zu empfehlen, weil sie durchaus mild ist und angenehm erfrischend wirkt. Man achte beim Einkauf genau auf die Firma und hüte sich vor wertlosen Nachahmungen. In allen besseren Parfümerie= und Drogen=Geschäften zum Preise von 50 Pfennig pro Stück zu haben. Wo nicht erhältlich, direkt durch die Fabrik von **Erdinger & Söhne, Bremen**

Wünschen Sie keine Gas-Rechnung

in beträchtlicher Höhe, so kochen Sie nur auf Rodensteins neuem Patent=Sparkocher „Monopol". Für jede Küche geeignet, ist der Kocher auch überall leicht anzubringen. Es wird nur zweidrittel soviel Gas verbraucht, wie mit anderen Apparaten bei gleicher Hitze=Entwickelung, auch fällt der lästige Gasgeruch vollständig fort. Verlangen Sie Prospekt mit genauer Beschreibung von **Max Rodenstein, Badstr.**

Reich ausgestattete Preislisten und Kataloge, sowie alle Arten von Drucksachen zu billigsten Preisen schnell und sauber bei E. Zander Charlottenburgerstr. 136

J·J·WEBER

Graphische Kunstanstalten

Telephon 19272-77 **LEIPZIG** Reudnitzer Straße 1–7

Anfertigung moderner Drucksachen, Prospekte, Kataloge u. Festschriften-Strich u. Autotypieklischees · Dreifarbenätzungen.

GIPKENS
Sarotti
HIMBEER-SCHOKOLADE
SAROTTI
HIMBEER=SCHOKOLADE
als Erfrischungs= und Stärkungsmittel
hat sich im Fluge die Gunst aller Sports=
leute erworben

ABCDEFGHI
HIJKLMMN
OOQRSTUV
WX · ij · p · qy̌ · YZ
Modern Schrift._bkl
amsu_vw_xyz.

Decoratie Schilders.&

bfkmnuvwxz gjpqyz

ABCEFGHIJJKLN

MORPTUVWXZ

abcdehilmostui

ABCDEGIJLOP
FHKMNQWI
RSTUVXY&
Zilversmidbh
aehou fktgyijqp.
wxz

GORKUMSCHE
FABRIEK
MOTHAERSUNDIL.
ABCDEFGHIJKLMN
OPRSTUVWXYZ.
WAGGERNOI

$6.50 48 Point 3 A 5 a

Simple 12
ENGLAND

$5.00 36 Point 4 A 6 a

Daily Test 4
BEST HOUSE

$4.00 24 Point 8 A 10 a

Maine & Boston 3
CHINESE LAUNDRY

$3.25 18 Point 11 A 16 a

Pleasant and Romantic $17
MOUNTAIN EXCURSIONS

Fonderie de Caractères d'Imprimerie Mayeur

Allainguillaume & Cie, Successeurs

LES MAURESQUES

Noires — PRIX PAR KILO — Blanches

1138 — Corps 9 — 12 fr. le kilo

Œuvres complètes d'Eugène Scribe, 86 Volumes
Belles Nouveautés de la Saison
EXPOSITION DE JOUETS POUR ENFANTS

Ces Caractères ont été gravés pour permettre l'emploi séparé de chacun des types ou pour être imprimés en couleurs par deux tirages retombant l'un sur l'autre à partir du Corps douze.

1139 — Corps 12 — 10 fr. | 1145 — Corps 12 — 10 fr.

Catalogue Général & Prix Courants | Catalogue Général & Prix Courants
CHAMPAGNE | SOIRÉE MUSICALE & DRAMATIQUE | CHAMPAGNE

1140 — Corps 18 — 8 fr. | 1146 — Corps 18 — 8 fr.

Les Volcans | Bières anglaises & françaises | Les Volcans
SPÉCIMENS 3460 | SPÉCIMENS 3460

1141 — Corps 24 — 7 fr. | 1147 — Corps 24 — 7 fr.

Chrysanthèmes | SPIRITUEUX | Chrysanthèmes
Accumulateurs Électriques

1142 — Corps 30 — 6 fr. 50 | 1148 — Corps 30 — 6 fr. 50

Revue historique | Revue historique
PARIS | AIX-LES-BAINS | PARIS

1143 — Corps 36 — 6 fr. | 1149 — Corps 36 — 6 fr.

Union | Cartes | Cartes | France
FORAINS | FORAINS

1144 — Corps 48 — 5 fr. 50 | 1150 — Corps 48 — 5 fr. 50

Pantomimes Burlesques
Caen | JOYEUX | Caen

Pages 239, 244 et 245 M réunies
3000 ex. — DÉPOSÉ

21, Rue du Montparnasse, à PARIS

ALLAINGUILLAUME & Cie
5-1904

G. B. BODONI

di Saluzzo 54

Arti GRAFICH

PROGRAMMA

Cic 5 - Classe A-l

Sommario!

Romualdo

ALBANESE

Cic. 10 - Classe A-i

Roha

LIBIA

Cic. 12 - Classe A-o

Sale

LIRE

FRANÇOIS NOULLARD
MEUBLES MODERNES
28, RUE GAILLON, PARIS

Ausstellung:
Korbmöbel u.
Leinenstickereien von
M. v. Brauchitsch-Mnchn.
Hohenzollern-
Kunstgewerbehaus
Friedmann & Weber
GIPKENS

FERDINAND GORMANNS NACHF.

FIRMEN-TAFELN IN GLAS, LACKIERTEM EISENBLECH ODER HARTHOLZ

KLOSTERNEUBURG
WERKSTÄTTE FÜR FIRMEN-SCHILDER, SCHRIFTEN- U. WAPPEN-MALEREI

PLASTISCHE BUCHSTABEN IN GLAS, BRONZE, BLECH GEGRÜNDET 1895

PORZELLAN-MANUFAKTUR KÖNIGSBERG

BRUNO PÜSCHEL

FAYENCEN, MARMOR-FIGUREN
GEFÄSSE IN ANTIKEN FORMEN

NIEDERLAGE: BERLIN
ORANIENSTRASSE 251

FEINES KRISTALL U. PORZELLAN
NACH KÜNSTLER-ENTWÜRFEN

GIRO-KONTO BEI DER
PREUSSISCHEN BANK

GRAPHISCHER KÜNSTLER-VEREIN KARLSRUHE

beehrt sich mit Gegenwärtigem, seinen werten Kollegen, Gönnern und Freunden von Karlsruhe und Umgegend ganz ergebenst anzuzeigen, daß die diesjährige Herbst-Ausstellung moderner Meister vom 25. Februar bis 30. März 1913 geöffnet ist. Die Ausstellung ist auch in diesem Jahre besonders reich beschickt worden und hoffen wir unsere Kunstfreunde recht zahlreich begrüßen zu dürfen

KARLSRUHE, Februar 1913 DAS AUSSTELLUNGS-KOMITEE

Ballo in Maschera

NOTIZIE ARIE

CORRIERINO

GIOPPINO & SO

Cic. 5 - Classe A-l

GIPKENS
HOHENZOLLERN KUNSTGEWERBE=
HAUS FRIEDMANN & WEBER
KÖNIGGRÄTZERSTR·8

4.–9. Oktober
Die Mode
für Herbst und Winter
Erste Ausstellung von
Original Pariser Modellen,
Paquin, Drecoll, Doucet,
Doeuillet, Hawet etc. im
Passage Kaufhaus
W. Wertheim G.m.b.H.
Friedrichstr. 110/112.
GIPKENS

AA DOMBURG

EFFECTENKANTOOR
ASSURANTIËN

TIJPOGRAPHIQUE

SPIRITUSFABRIEK
DE STER

NEDERLANDSCHE
BANK

BLOEMEN-
MAGAZIJN

MABLURPAEAMDRRU

DTRGEHAFFEROOCHEI

ROMARAEDAR

EBAINRAAVAH

AUDOH VANDIJK

SCHEULOOSM LEONARDUS

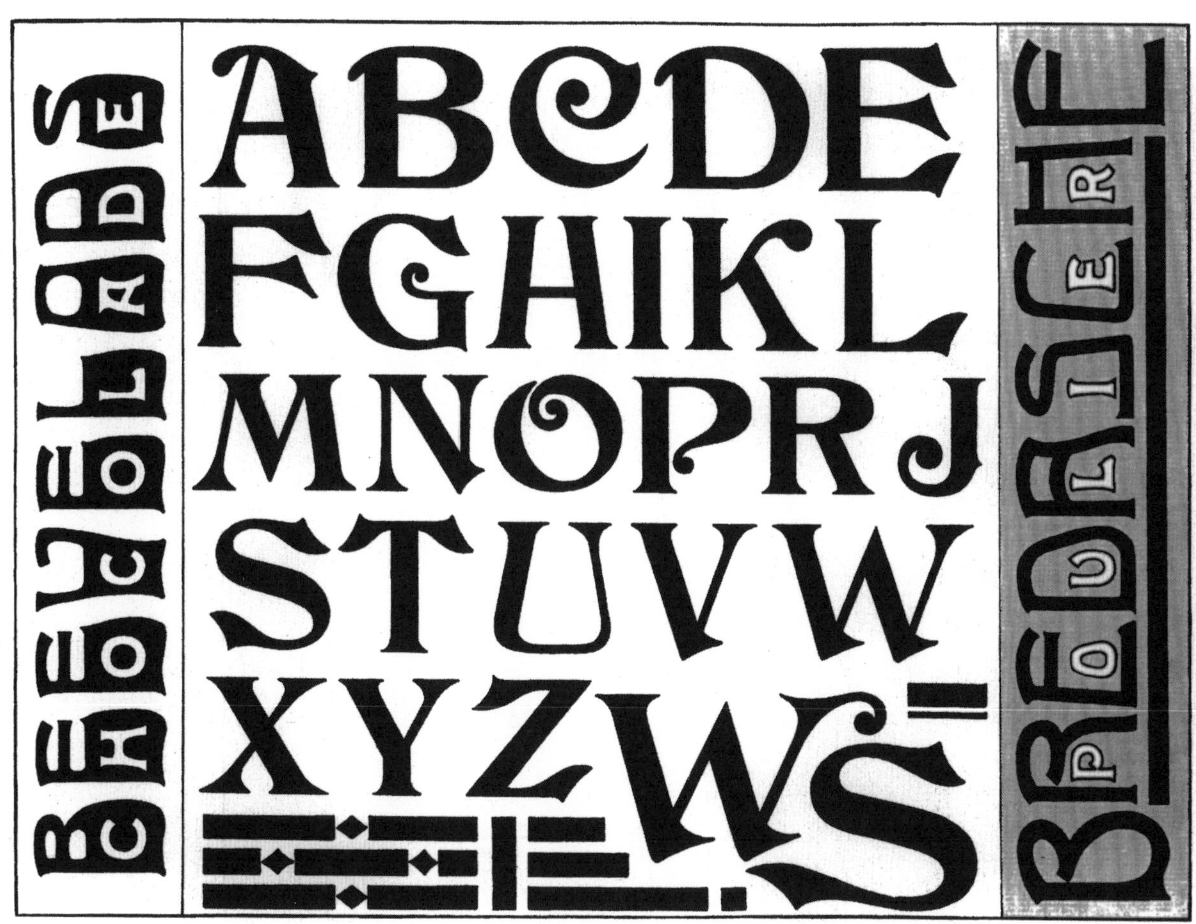
ABCDE
FGHIKL
MNOPRJ
STUVW
XYZ

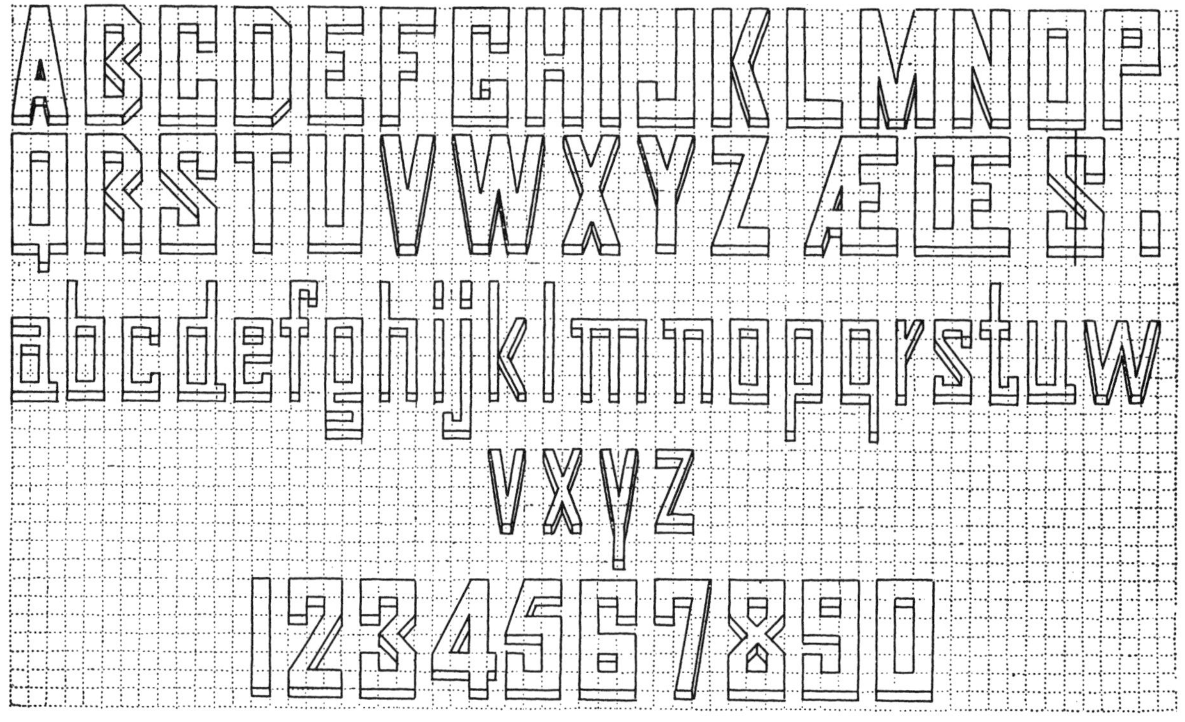

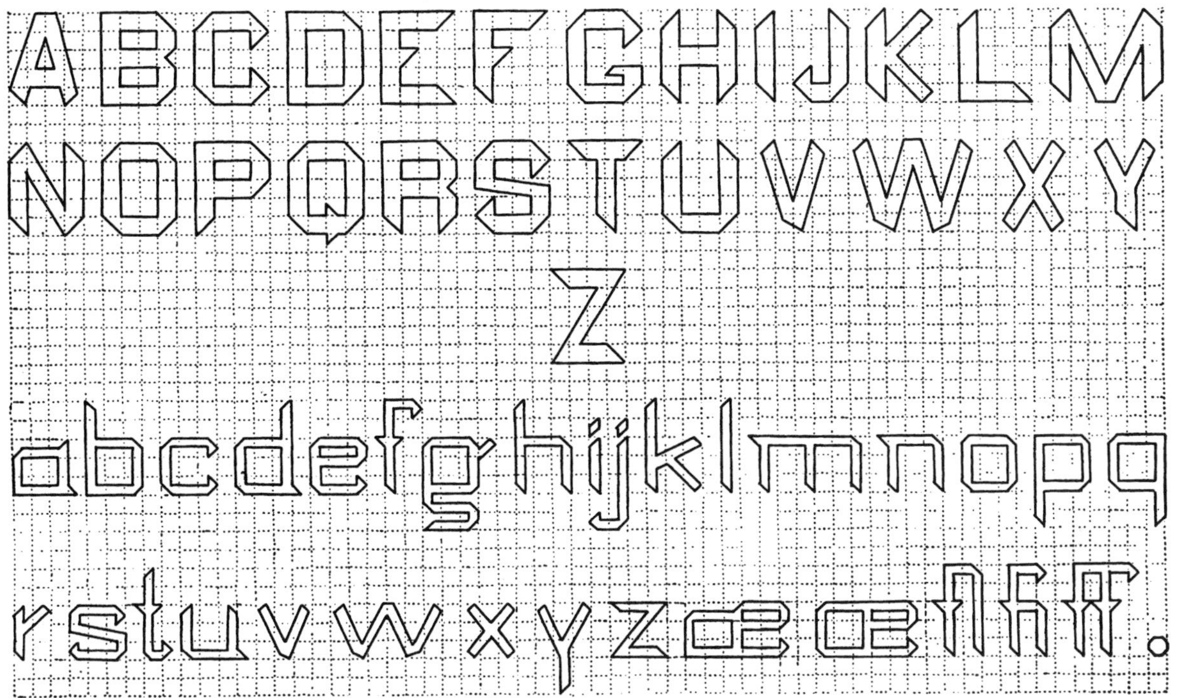

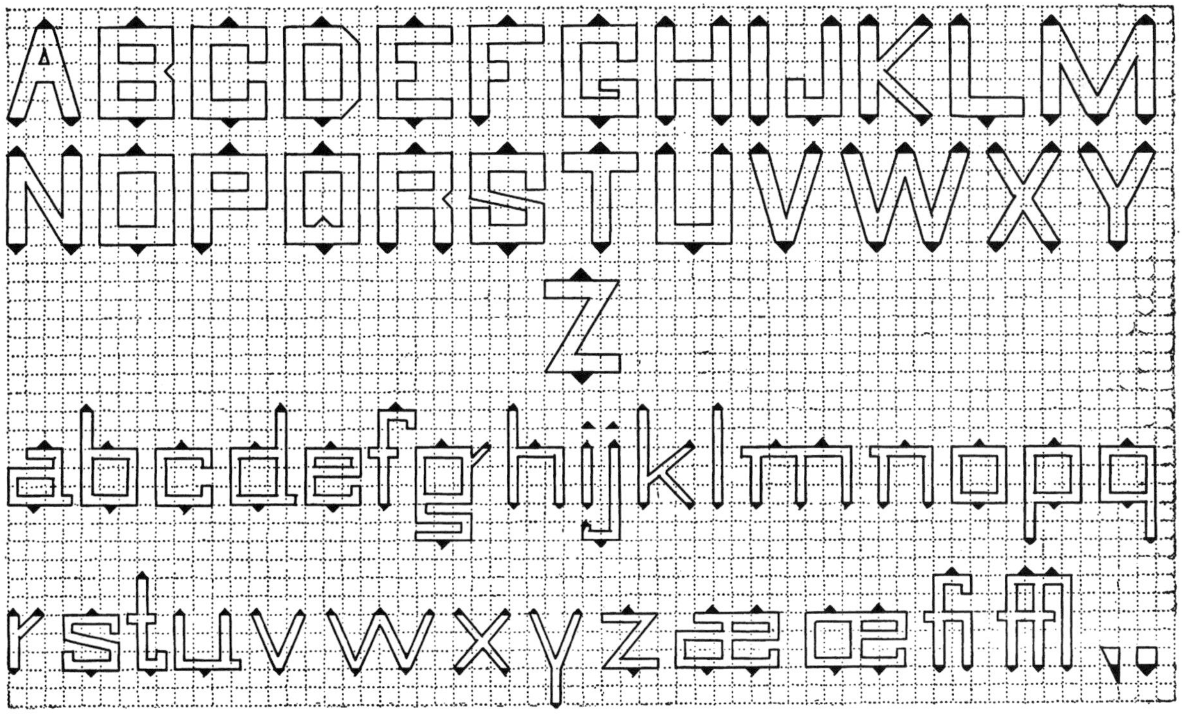

N.V. DE ARBEIDERSPERS
N.V. DE ARBEIDERSPERS
N.V. DE ARBEIDERSPERS
N.V. DE ARBEIDERSPERS
N.V. DE ARBEIDERSPERS
N.V. DE ARBEIDERSPERS
FILM- EN
RASTERPROEVEN
HEKELVELD 15, AMSTERDAM, TEL. 32600
HEKELVELD 15, AMSTERDAM, TEL. 32600
HEKELVELD 15, AMSTERDAM, TEL. 32600
HEKELVELD 15, AMSTERDAM, TEL. 32600
HEKELVELD 15, AMSTERDAM, TEL. 32600
HEKELVELD 15, AMSTERDAM, TEL. 32600

BETONBOUW-MAATSCHAPPIJ

TELEFOON 28543

Ontwerpers en uitvoerders van bouwwerken in gewapend beton, als Fabrieken, Bruggen, Sluizen, Havenhoofden, Kademuren, enz.

HUGO DE GROOTSTRAAT 159 · ROTTERDAM

Transito en Nobel-Antieke

BOUVY & ZONEN

AAST 'T FIJNE porselein, linnen en zilver, verleent het glaswerk aan de gedekte tafel haar bijzonder cachet. Behalve aan de door het gebruik gestelde eischen moet het ook voldoen aan schoonheidseischen en het behoort een sieraad voor de tafel te zijn. De vorm der glazen moet tot een gullen dronk nooden. Wie ons glaswerk koopt is ervan verzekerd zijn gasten het beste voor te zetten.

NEUDE 15-17 UTRECHT

WAT 1933 BRENGEN ZAL ?

Niemand weet het, maar laten we vooral niet pessimistisch zijn! Laten we ons schrap zetten tegen alles wat ons verder naar beneden kan trekken.
„How to make the best of it", moet in 1933 ons devies zijn. In beweging blijven, want door die beweging ontstaat de opening die terugvoert naar het normale zakenleven.
Deze beweging vindt U ook in het maandblad De Organisator, met zijn pittigen, rijken en zakelijken inhoud. Het is vol ideeën, die slechts wachten op toepassing.

STIMULEEREND
PITTIG
ZAKELIJK

Abonnement: f 6.- per jaar (12 nummers). 50 cent per nummer.

UITKNIPPEN

Aan de **ORGANISATOR, COOLSINGEL 79, ROTTERDAM.**

Verzoeke abonnement/proefnummer voor:

Naam ....

te .... *adres* ....

Voor proefno. 25 ct. postzegels insluiten 5

Cic. 12 - Classe B-l

Serie SVEZIA

GIRLS

Cic. 18 - Classe C-g

Cic. 20 - Classe C-n

LEO

[71]

BDG
Blätter
MITTEILUNGEN
DES BUNDES
DEUTSCHER
GEBRAUCHS-
GRAPHIKER·E·V·
JAHRG. 1927 HEFT 1
Als Manuscript gedruckt.

UNSER
INVENTUR-
AUSVERKAUF
HAT BEGONNEN
Auf alle Waren
20
Prozent Rabatt
MODENHAUS
SCHLESINGER

Serie »Göppingen« Nr. 114

Graue Linie 868

Telephonzeichen 1254

Kaffee
Kakao
billiger!
HANS KORN
Friedrichsplatz 2

Handschriftliche Linie 1029

Weights and Prices given are Approximate; see page 2. Cast on Uniform Line.

5 A 8 a	36 Point Sheridan	8⅜ lbs., **$5.20**

NORTON AVENUE
Evanston Club 68 Rooms

5 A 7 a	48 Point Sheridan	12 9/16 lbs., **$7.70**

FOUNDATIONS
Wholesale 34 House

3 A 4 a	60 Point Sheridan	14 1/16 lbs., **$8.40**

AMERICAN
Sand 94 Banks

3 A 3 a	72 Point Sheridan	16½ lbs., **$9.55**

MODERN
Auditorium 8

POINT-LINE, POINT-SET, POINT-BODY 405 QUALITY AND FINISH UNEQUALED

PLYMOUTH [SUPERIOR COPPER MIXED TYPE — POINT LINE POINT SET POINT BODY] ITALIC

Weights and Prices given are Approximate; see page 2. Cast on Uniform Line.

3A 4a — 36 Point Plymouth Italic — 8 5/16 lbs., **$5.20**

ROSE BUSH
Fragrant 4 Flowers

3A 4a — 48 Point Plymouth Italic — 13 3/16 lbs., **$7.90**

GENVINE
Rhine 6 Stones

3A 4a — 60 Point Plymouth Italic — 18 3/4 lbs., **$11.25**

BONDS
Large 3 Duck

3A 3a — 72 Point Plymouth Italic — 19 5/8 lbs., **$11.40**

SHINE
Long 5 Run

$11.00 48 Point 4 A 5 a

GO Mit 2

$8.50 36 Point 4 A 6 a

Sails Far 3
BOAT RIO

$5.00 24 Point 6 A 8 a

Ocean Travels 4
CHURCH CHOIR

$4.50 18 Point 8 A 10 a

Improved Property 5
ARTISTIC PICTURE

$3.25 12 Point 14 A 16 a

Antiquarian Among Books $67
HAVE SUITED HUNDREDS

$3.00 10 Point 14 A 18 a

Books Contain Valuable Information 89
THE RARE MOUNTAIN FLOWER

MARTE

GIOVE!

Cic. 12 - Classe B-l

Metro

REMO

$11.90 60 Point 3 A 4 a

Horned 5

$9.25 48 Point 3 A 5 a

3 Milestone
Landmarks

$7.50 36 Point 3 A 7 a

Winter 4 Game
Hiding

$4.50 24 Point 4 A 10 a

Standard Editorials
Writers 6 Magazine

DEARBORN INITIALS

Cast from Superior Copper-Mixed Metal.

Per set of one each, $1.00 — 24 Point Dearborn Initials — Single characters, 10c

A	B	C	D	E	F	G
H	I	J	K	L	M	N
O	P	Q	R	S	T	
U	V	W	X	Y	Z	

INITIALS MORTISED

Per set of one each, $1.50 — 36 Point Dearborn Initials — Single characters, 15c

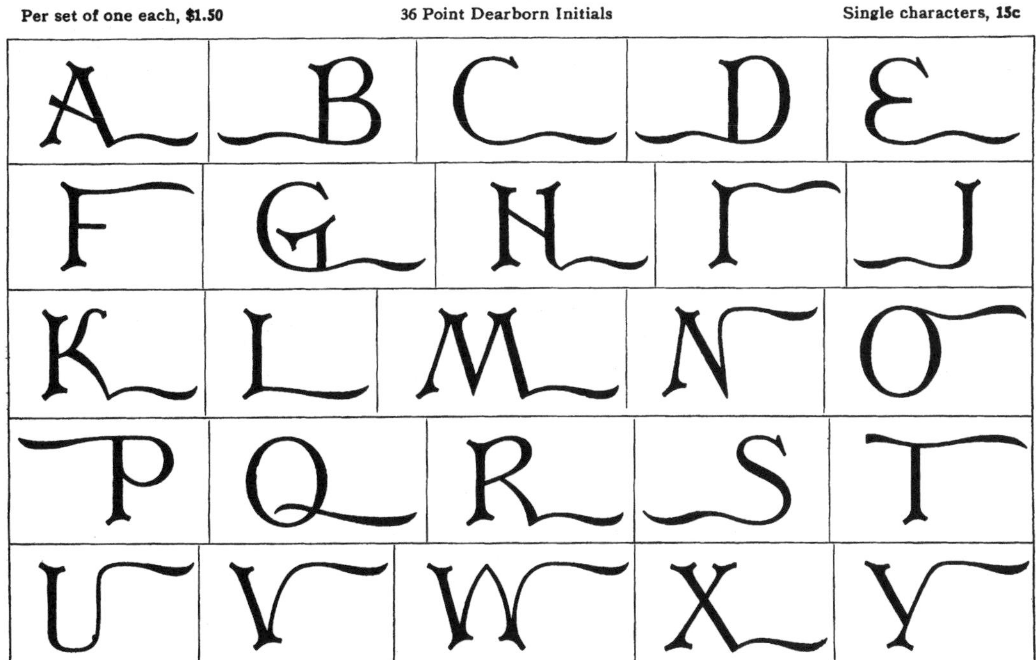

DESCRIPTIVE CATALOGUE

OF

Hot Water Heaters,

Steam Heaters,

AN

COMBINATION

Hot Water and Warm Air Furnaces,

MANUFACTURED BY

FULLER & WARREN COMPANY,

Troy, N. Y., *Milwaukee,* *Chicago,* *Cleveland,*

New York, *Boston.*

MERCUUR-STOOMDRUKKERIJ
J. H. DE BUSSY ✠ ✠ ✠ ✠ AMSTERDAM
ROKIN 60—62 EN RUSTENBURGERSTRAAT 148.

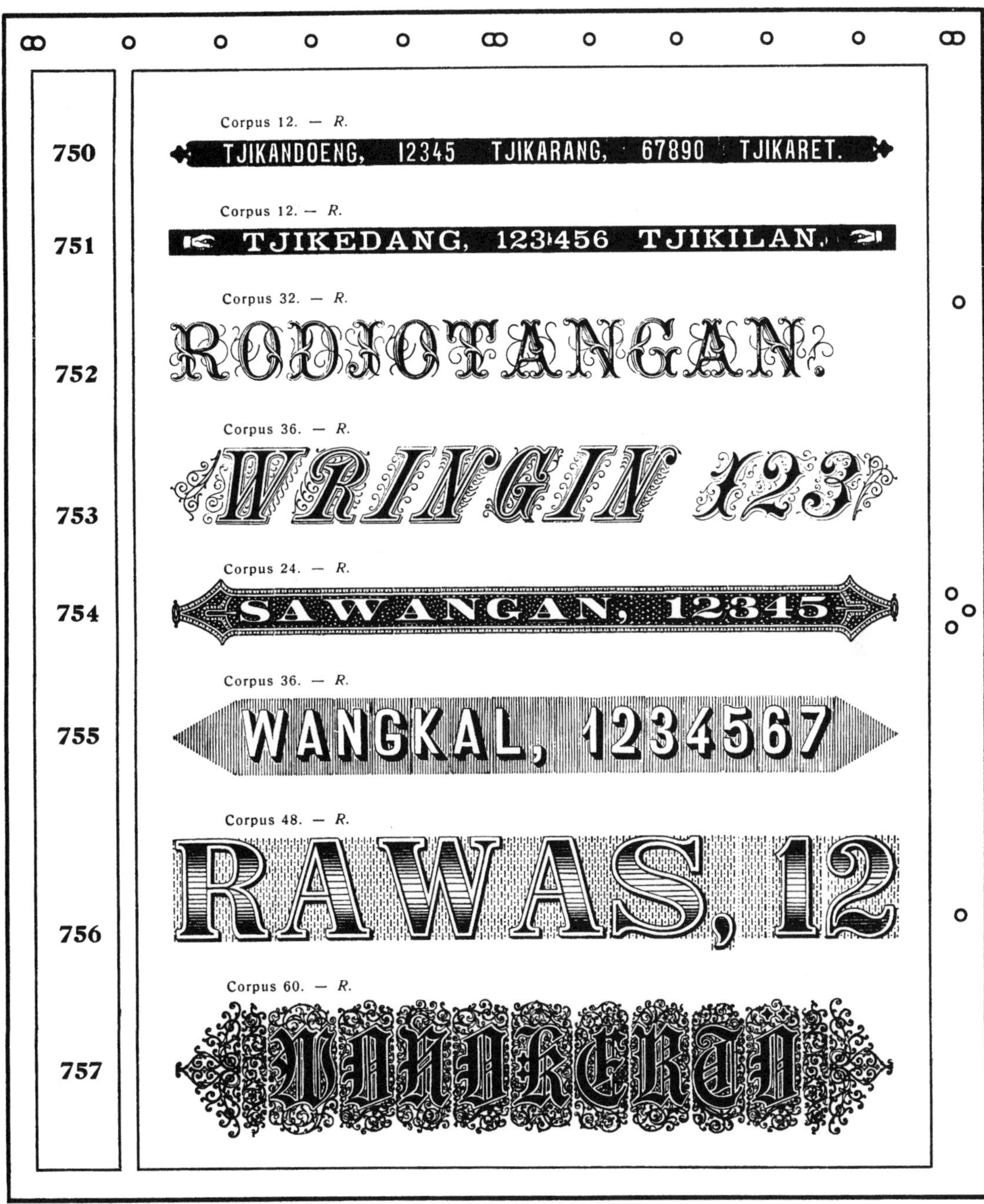

TWENTY LINES GILL SANS INLINED

MS

SIXTEEN LINES GILL SANS INLINED

DIG

TEN LINES GILL SANS INLINED

BORE

OTHER SIZES SUPPLIED WITH EQUAL FACILITY

339

STEPHENSON, BLAKE & CO. LIMITED SHEFFIELD, LONDON, MANCHESTER

N. 1655 - Corpo 12 (Genio) Kg. 2,50 (A-40)

ITALIA DANIMARCA MONTENEGRO

N. 1656 - Corpo 18 (Genziana) Kg. 3,– (A-16)

STABILIMENTI GRAFICI

N. 1657 - Corpo 24 (Geografo) Kg. 3,75 (A-12)

FOTOTIPOGRAFIA

N. 1658 - Corpo 36 (Geometra) Kg. 5,– (A-6)

AEROPLANO

Tacca Francese CARATTERI NICOLA *Classe **D***

N. 1763 - Corpo 18 (Idra) Kg. 3,50 (A-16)

INGLORIOSAMENTE

N. 1764 - Corpo 24 (Idraulico) Kg. 4,50 (A-12)

INTERPRETARE

N. 1765 - Corpo 28 (Idrofobia) Kg. 4,50 (A-8)

MONTANARI

N. 1766 - Corpo 36 (Idrogeno) Kg. 5,50 (A-6)

CENTAURI

Le CLAIR DE LUNE LARGE

Corps 60

ABCDEFGH
IJKLMNOPQ
RSTUVXYZ!
ÆŒWÇÉÈ?
Ê&&c.&.',;:()-
abcdefghijkl
mnopqrstuv
xyzæœwçéà
1234567890

FANTASQUES-LARGES

Corps 60

ABCDE

FGHIJ

KLMN

OPQRS

TUVX

YZÉÈÊ

ÆŒW

Ç &

ROBERT HAAS
SECESSION
SONDER
AUSSTELLUNG
MIT KOLLEKTIONEN:
FRIEDRICH KÖNIG · JOSEF
ENGELHART · HEINR. KRAUSE
MAXIMILIAN LENZ · CARL
MÜLLER · DR. ALFRED PÖLL
1. JUNI – 31. JULI 1929

FRANKFURT'M
C. NAUMANN'S
DRUCKEREI
Wir pflegen den guten Offsetdruck, Tiefdruck, Buchdruck u. Steindruck • Durch die modernste Einrichtung sind wir in der Lage die höchsten Anförderungen in Qualität und Leistung zu erfüllen •
BPG

ORNAMENT

DECORATION HAS LONG BEEN CENTRAL TO ALL KINDS OF DESIGN, REGARDLESS OF WHETHER IT IS TWO OR THREE dimensions. Designers have had passions either for or against it. For some, it is sublime; for others, it is a crime. Hot-metal type foundries were the great purveyors of decorative material, providing pounds of the stuff to printers large and small. Until the European Modern movement of the early 1920s and its typographic wing known as the New Typography banished ornamental typographic devices from contemporary graphic design, decorative borders and initial capitals were a primary element of the printer's visual lexicon.

Yet throughout, the vocabulary of ornament stylistic distinctions apply—indeed some are more decadent than others. Like architecture, the use of decorative material is determined by the aesthetic essence of the structure. A page that employs Art Nouveau lettering is sympathetic to naturalistic, curvilinear ornament, while one that uses Modernistic (or Art Deco) type calls for rectilinear dingbats and fleurons. Type designers of the past have devoted almost as much time to creating families of borders, cornices, and frames as typefaces. No printer or designer would dare use a passé ornamental device lest he be accused of being déclassé.

Although today's digital decorative concoctions are numerous, they are not surpassed in quantity (or quality) by the exuberant and fanciful ornaments of earlier times. There was no stopping the anonymous craftspersons who arduously engraved the intricate designs, meandering patterns, and eccentric arabesques.

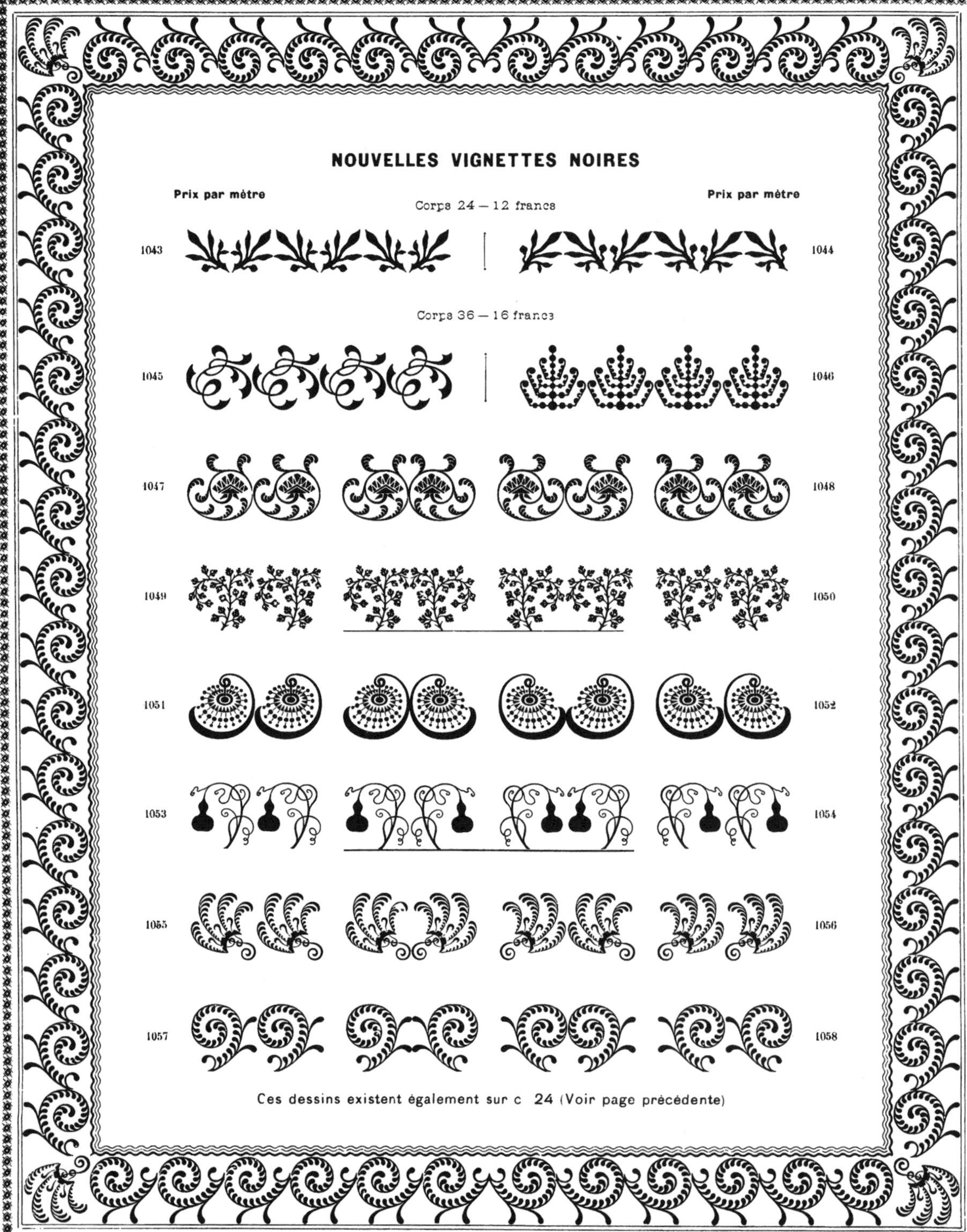

NOUVELLES VIGNETTES NOIRES

Prix par mètre | **Prix par mètre**

Corps 24 — 12 francs

1043 | 1044

Corps 36 — 16 francs

1045 | 1046

1047 | 1048

1049 | 1050

1051 | 1052

1053 | 1054

1055 | 1056

1057 | 1058

Ces dessins existent également sur c 24 (Voir page précédente)

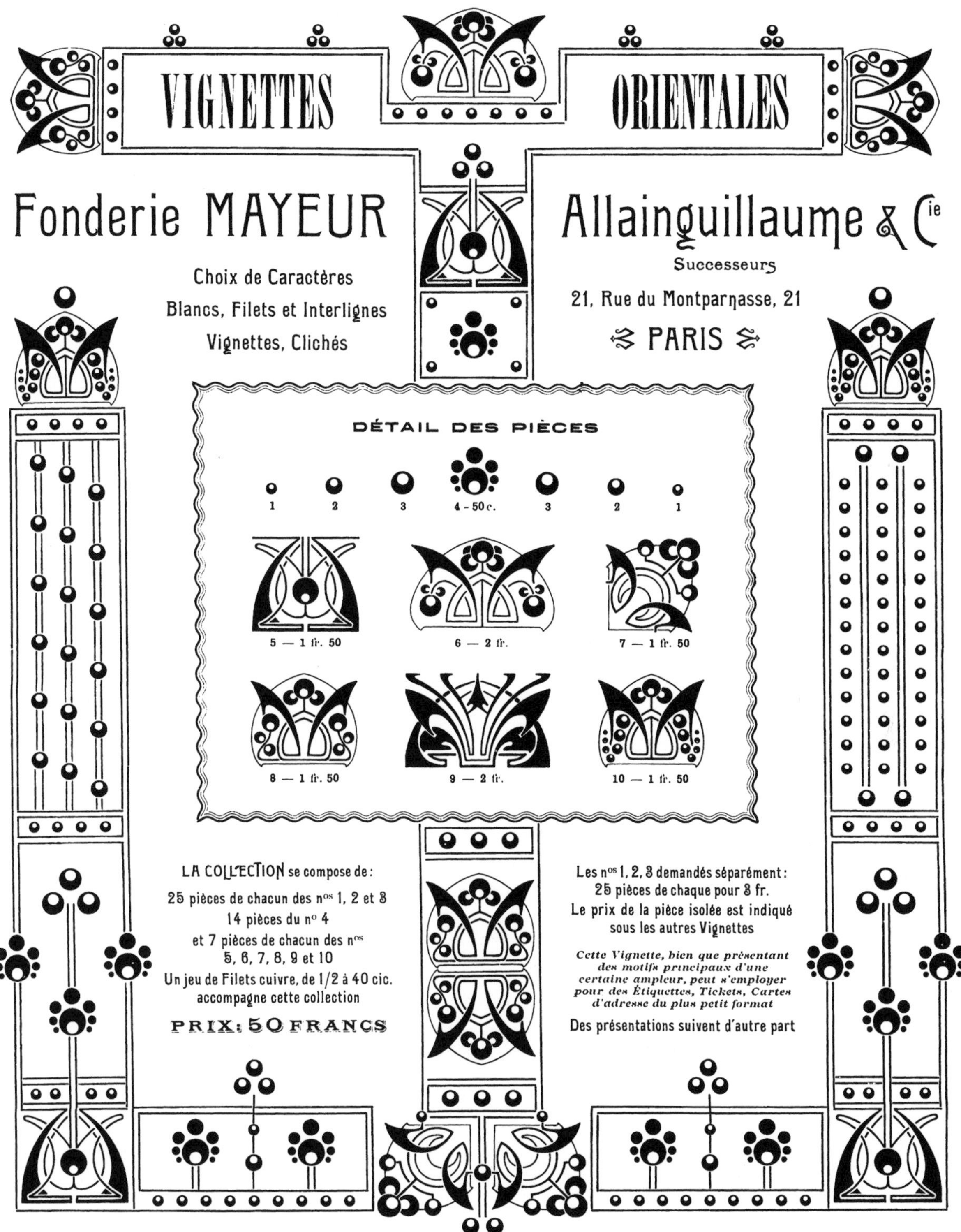
VIGNETTES ORIENTALES
Fonderie MAYEUR
Choix de Caractères
Blancs, Filets et Interlignes
Vignettes, Clichés
Allainguillaume & Cie
Successeurs
21, Rue du Montparnasse, 21
PARIS
DÉTAIL DES PIÈCES
1
2
3
4 - 50 c.
3
2
1
5 — 1 fr. 50
6 — 2 fr.
7 — 1 fr. 50
8 — 1 fr. 50
9 — 2 fr.
10 — 1 fr. 50
LA COLLECTION se compose de :
25 pièces de chacun des nos 1, 2 et 3
14 pièces du no 4
et 7 pièces de chacun des nos
5, 6, 7, 8, 9 et 10
Un jeu de Filets cuivre, de 1/2 à 40 cic.
accompagne cette collection
PRIX: 50 FRANCS
Les nos 1, 2, 3 demandés séparément :
25 pièces de chaque pour 3 fr.
Le prix de la pièce isolée est indiqué
sous les autres Vignettes
Cette Vignette, bien que présentant
des motifs principaux d'une
certaine ampleur, peut s'employer
pour des Étiquettes, Tickets, Cartes
d'adresse du plus petit format
Des présentations suivent d'autre part

Züge und Ansatzstücke zur Kalligraphia

auf Seite 630—631

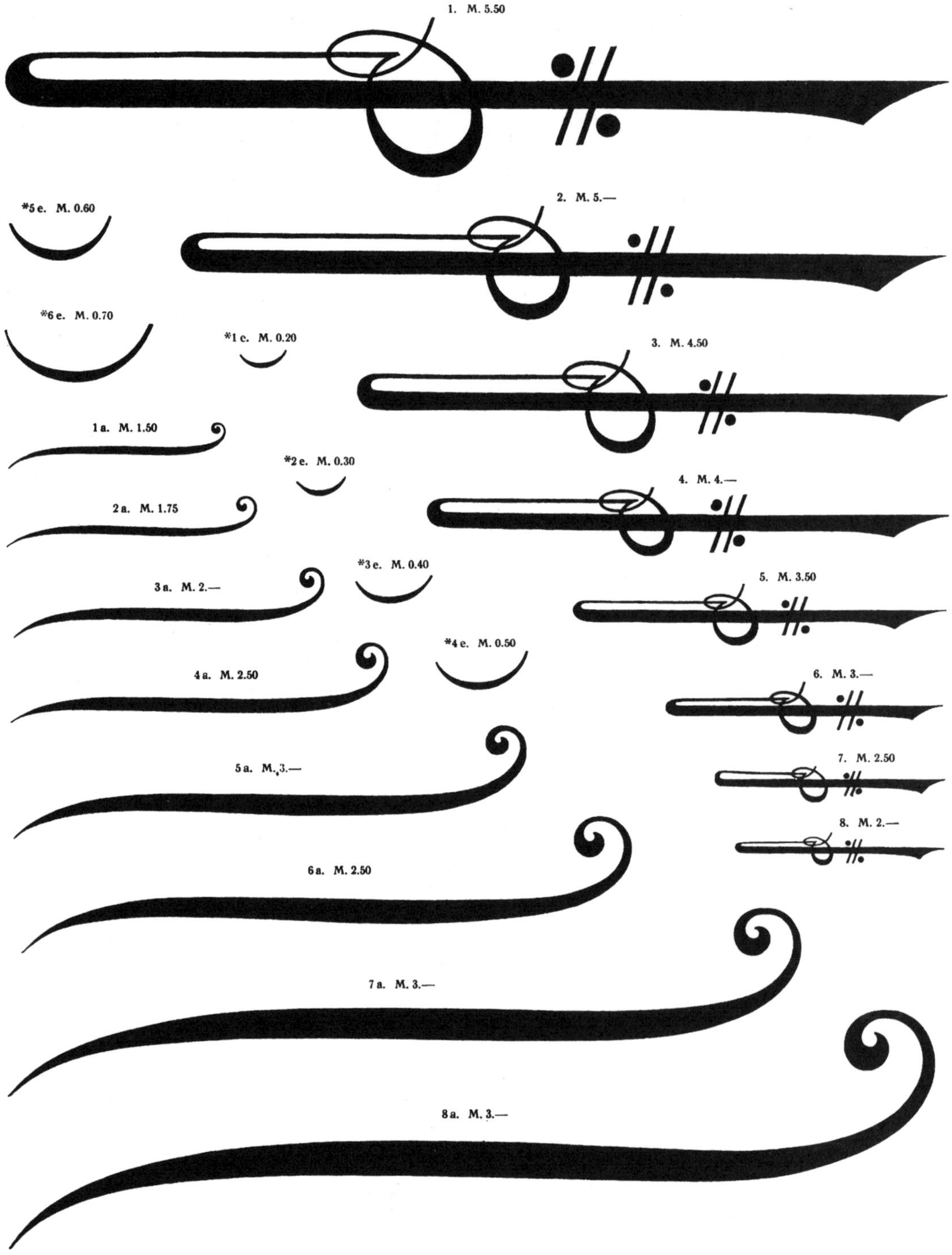

Züge und Ansatzstücke zur Kalligraphia

auf Seite 630—631

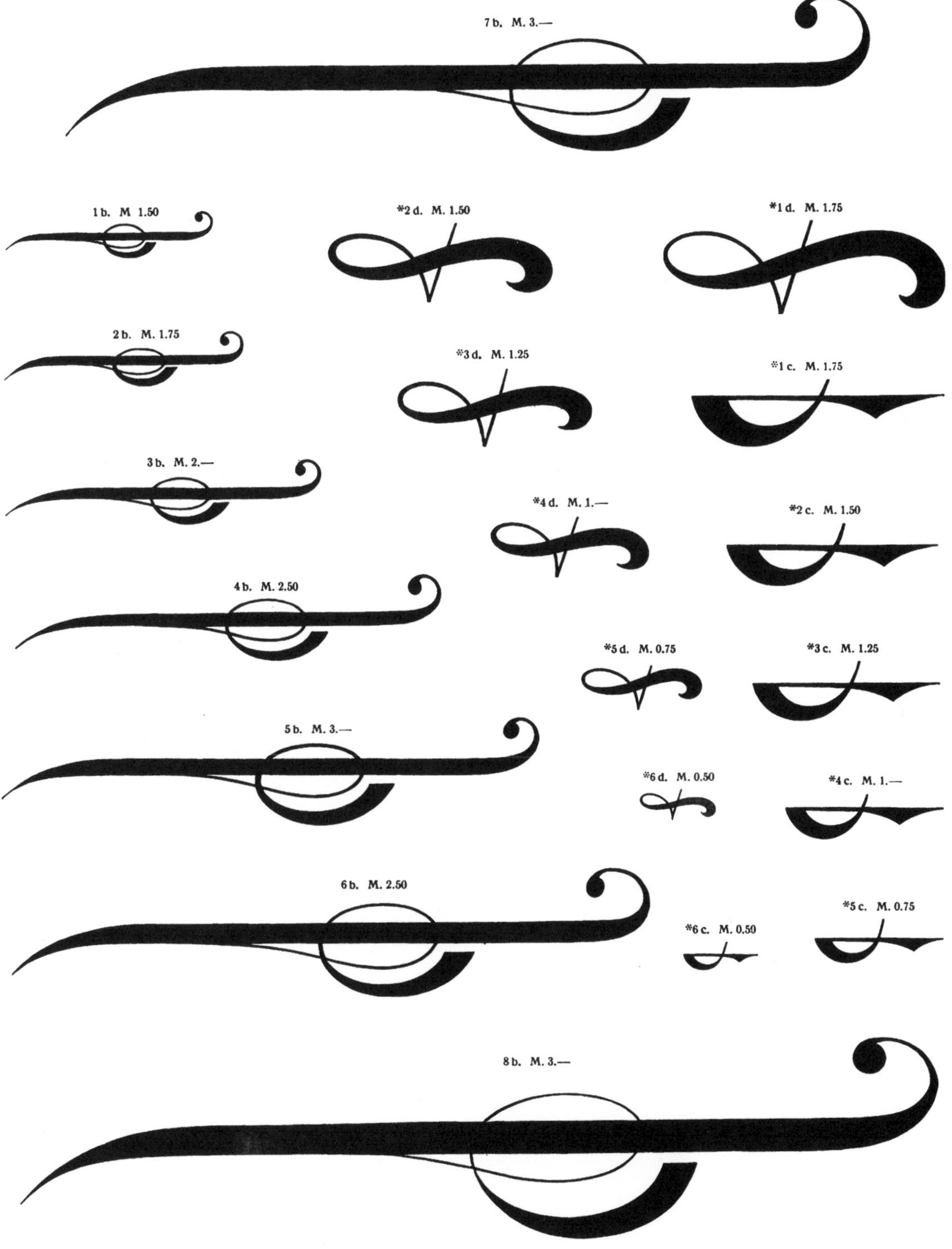

AMSTEL-RANDEN

Corps 48. Minimum 8 Kg.

56

57

58

59

60

Corps 60. Minimum 10 Kg.

61

62

N.V. LETTERGIETERIJ ‚AMSTERDAM' VOORH. N. TETTERODE

ZWART-GRIJS RANDEN

No. 1 Minimum 2 Kg. Corps 12

No. 2 Minimum 2 Kg. Corps 12

No. 3 Minimum 2 Kg. Corps 12

No. 4 Minimum 3 Kg. Corps 18

No. 5 Minimum 3 Kg. Corps 18

No. 6 Minimum 3 Kg. Corps 18

No. 7 Minimum 4 Kg. Corps 24

No. 8 Minimum 4 Kg. Corps 24

No. 9 Minimum 4 Kg. Corps 24

N. V. LETTERGIETERIJ „AMSTERDAM" VOORH. N. TETTERODE

SÉCURITÉ
PUNAISES EN ACIER
MADOU - BRUXELLES

H

R

Q

M

S

C
S
A

B
G

N

W

FINIS

A

SOCIETÀ AUGUSTA  TORINO (ITALIA)

FREGIO SERIE 36 U.

PARTE PRIMA (Savio) Minimo Kg. 12 Fr. **100**

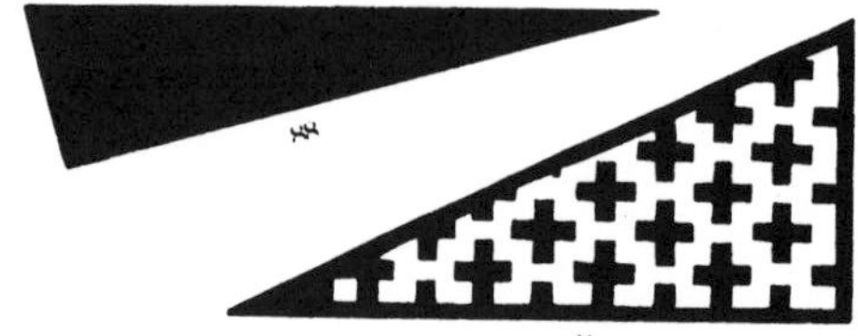

Linien für Inserat-Einfassungen

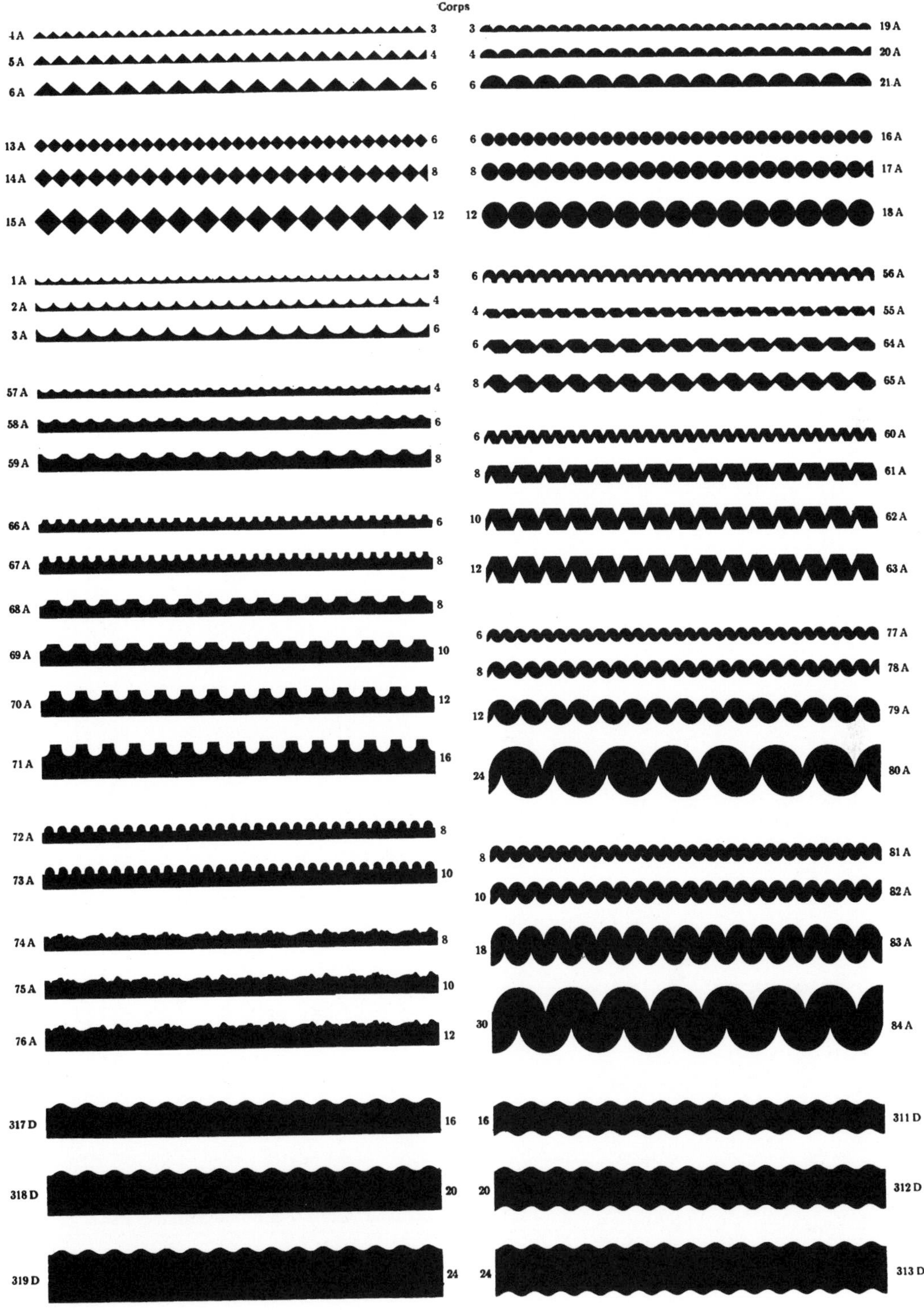

TEMPLE  ORNAMENTS

Cast from Superior Copper-Mixed Metal.

1018-60c

1020-60c

1019-60c

1027-60c

1016-60c

1023-75c

1015-60c

1028-60c

1021-60c

1017-60c

1022-60c

1026-50c

1024-75c

1025-75c

Above prices include two of each Cap and Base.

ORIGINAL

FIGUREN DER PLAKETTE

GESCHÜTZT

SERIE 669

TEIL D. Min. ca. 20 kg

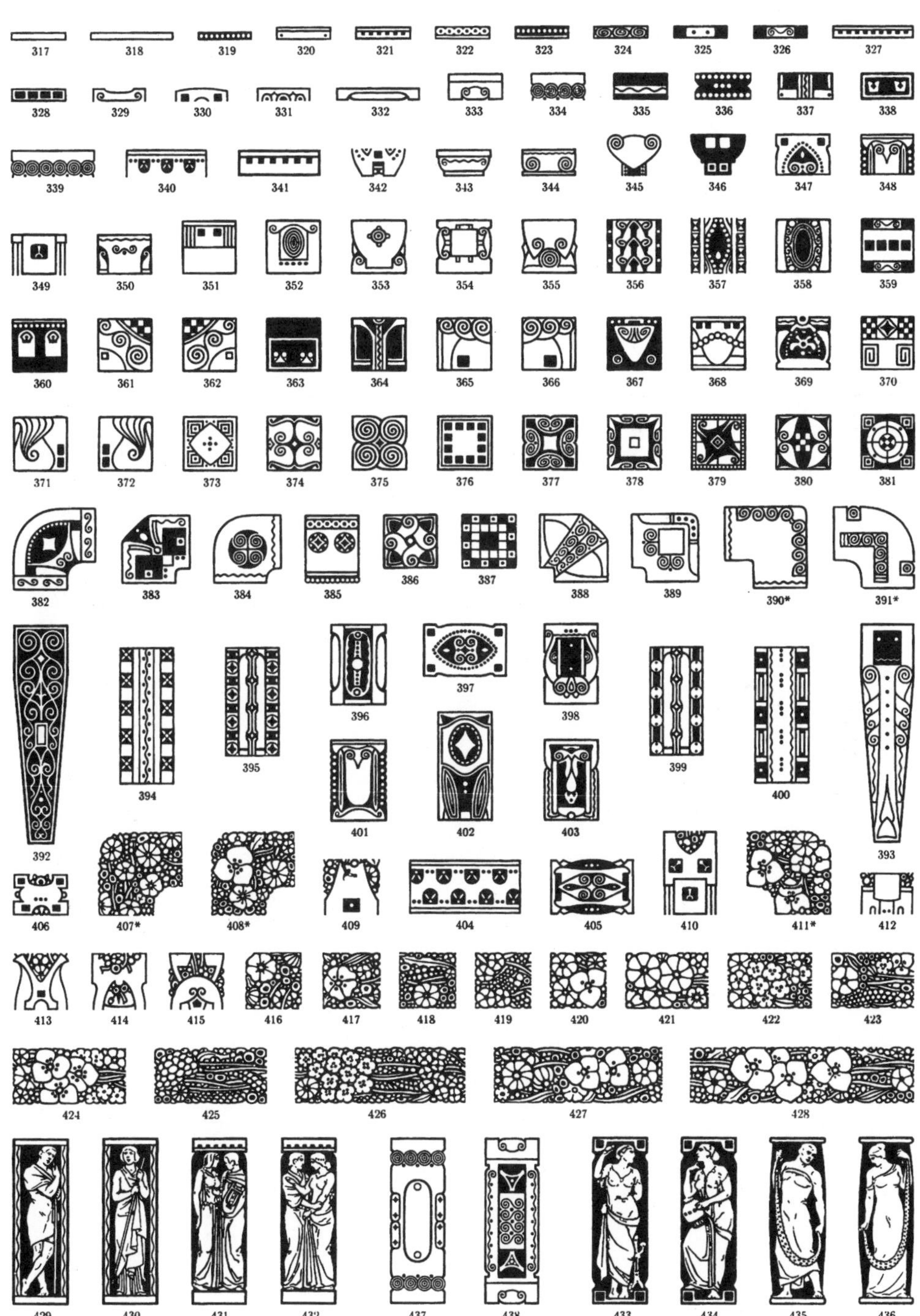

Augsburger Initialen und Ornamente

1366 a. Corps 36. 1 Alphabet M. 20.—, einzeln das Stück M. 1.—

Initial-Ornamente zu No. 1366 a. 1 Sortiment M. 14.50, 1/2 Sortiment M. 7.75

No. 5. M. 1.50

No. 6. M. 1.—

No. 7. M. —.60

No. 8. M. —.30

1367 a. Corps 72. 1 Alphabet M. 40.—, einzeln das Stück M. 2.25

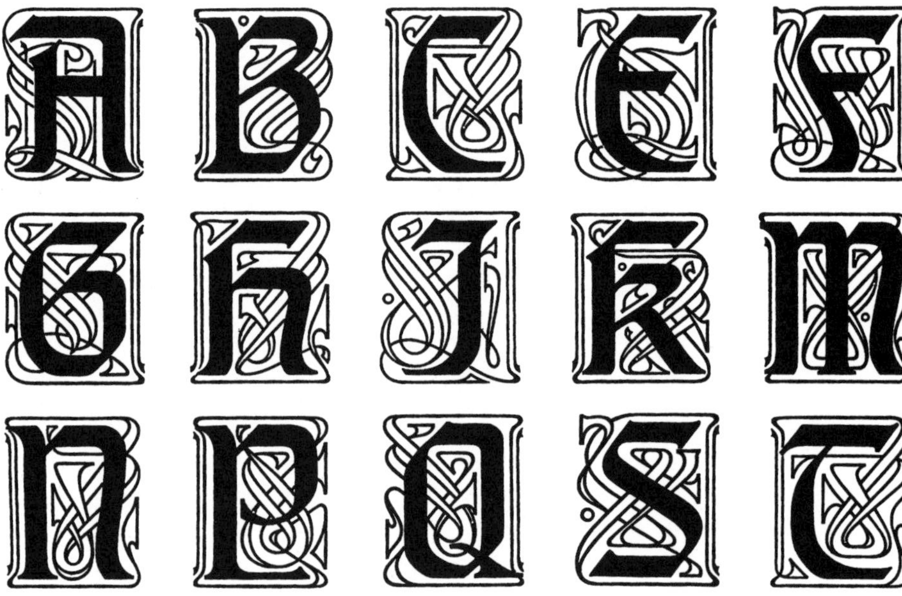

Initial-Ornamente zu No. 1367 a. 1 Sortiment M. 22.—, 1/2 Sortiment M. 12.—

No. 9. M. 3.20

No. 11. M. 1.35

No. 12. M. —.70

No. 10. M. 2.25

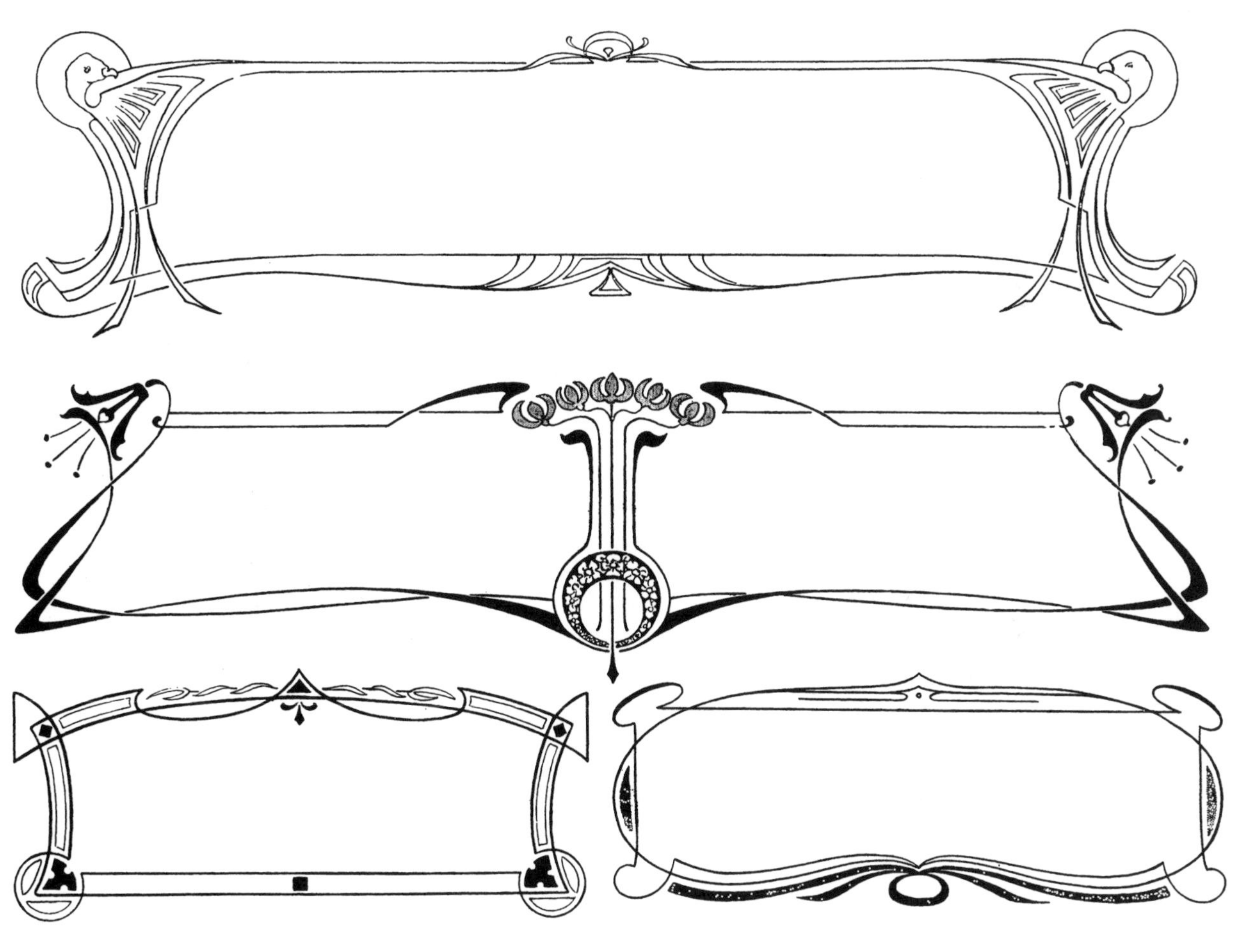

Compositions établies
avec la DEUXIÈME COLLECTION
des ORNEMENTS JAPONAIS
Composée de 196 pièces
PRIX : 55 FRANCS
dont les dessins figurent page 304 ci-devant
MÉDAILLE D'OR
PARIS 1900
Caractères d'Imprimerie
MAYEUR
Allainguillaume & Cie
Successeurs
21, Rue du Montparnasse
PARIS
TÉLÉPHONE
704-59
Adresse Télégraphique :
Mayeur-Montparnasse-Paris
BEAU CHOIX DE CARACTÈRES
VIGNETTES
FILETS ET INTERLIGNES
SYSTÉMATIQUES
BLANCS, GARNITURES
& LINGOTS
POUDRE
DE RIZ
RIGO
extra
1 fr. 50 la boîte
PHARMACIE
Gressier
8, rue Basse
BERNAY
DROGUERIE
ANALYSES
Hôtel du Luxembourg
SALONS POUR NOCES & BANQUETS
E. Marinier
MAITRE-D'HOTEL
28, Avenue Victor Hugo
SAINT-LO
BILLARD
Estaminet
à 5 minutes
de la Gare

Les corps inférieurs & supérieurs sont en gravure

Les LATINES INCRUSTÉES avec bas de casse

1281 — Corps 18 — 10 fr. le kilo

Les Halles de Paris

QUELQUES NOUVEAUTÉS en préparation

1282 — Corps 24 — 9 fr.

Circonférence

1283 — Corps 30 — 8 fr. 50

Automobile

1281 — Corps 18 — 10 fr.

LYON BORDEAUX

1282 — Corps 24 — 9 fr.

BAL DE NUIT

MM. les Imprimeurs qui possèdent les Initiales de ce Caractère sont informés que les Lettres de la nouvelle gravure bas de casse sont fondues sur le même alignement que ces Initiales.

1283 — Corps 30 — 8 fr. 50

MAI JUIN

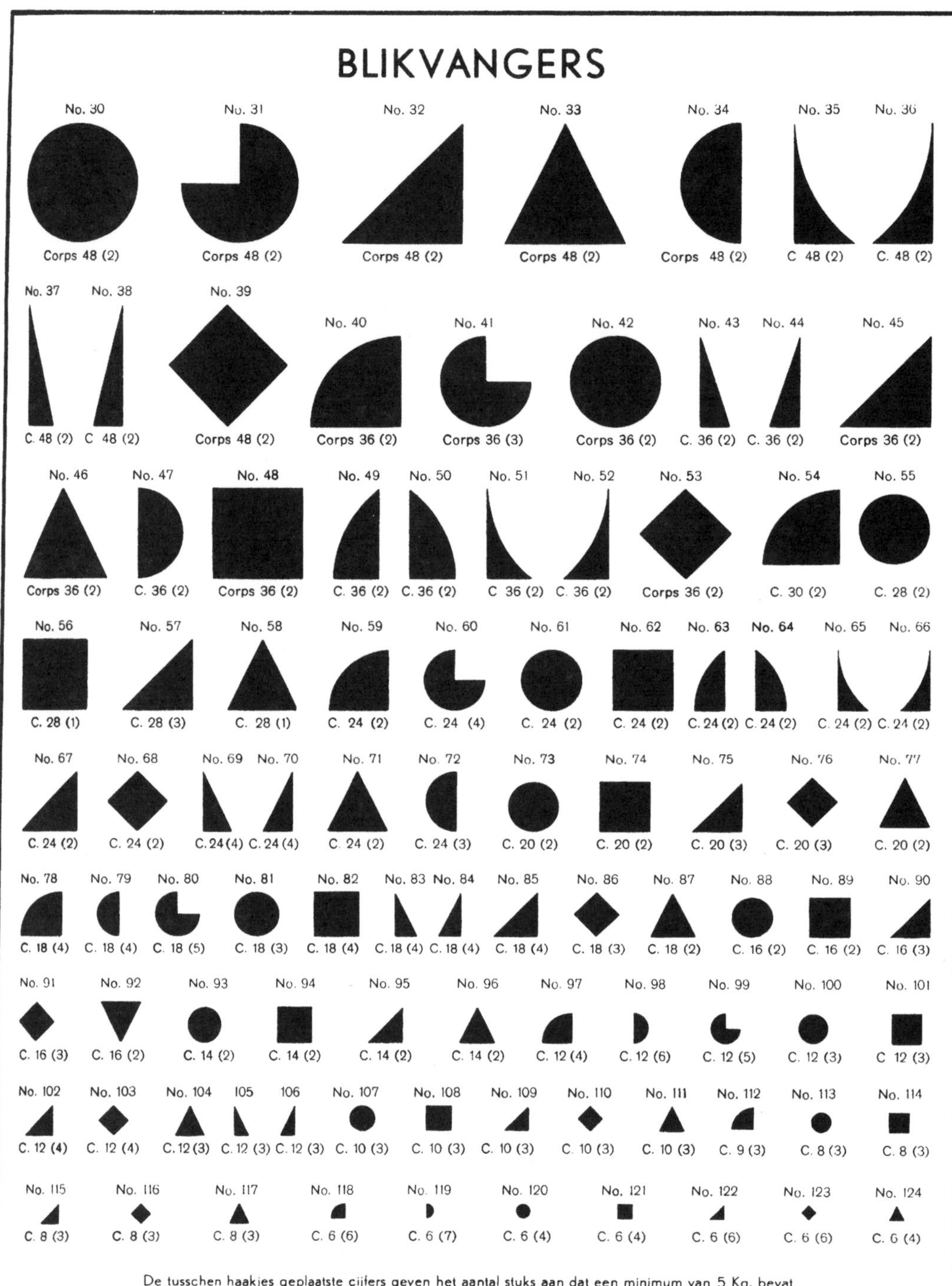

BLIKVANGERS

No. 30 | No. 31 | No. 32 | No. 33 | No. 34 | No. 35 | No. 36
Corps 48 (2) | Corps 48 (2) | Corps 48 (2) | Corps 48 (2) | Corps 48 (2) | C 48 (2) | C. 48 (2)

No. 37 | No. 38 | No. 39 | No. 40 | No. 41 | No. 42 | No. 43 | No. 44 | No. 45
C. 48 (2) | C 48 (2) | Corps 48 (2) | Corps 36 (2) | Corps 36 (3) | Corps 36 (2) | C. 36 (2) | C. 36 (2) | Corps 36 (2)

No. 46 | No. 47 | No. 48 | No. 49 | No. 50 | No. 51 | No. 52 | No. 53 | No. 54 | No. 55
Corps 36 (2) | C. 36 (2) | Corps 36 (2) | C. 36 (2) | C. 36 (2) | C 36 (2) | C. 36 (2) | Corps 36 (2) | C. 30 (2) | C. 28 (2)

No. 56 | No. 57 | No. 58 | No. 59 | No. 60 | No. 61 | No. 62 | No. 63 | No. 64 | No. 65 | No. 66
C. 28 (1) | C. 28 (3) | C. 28 (1) | C. 24 (2) | C. 24 (4) | C. 24 (2) | C. 24 (2) | C. 24 (2) | C. 24 (2) | C. 24 (2) | C. 24 (2)

No. 67 | No. 68 | No. 69 | No. 70 | No. 71 | No. 72 | No. 73 | No. 74 | No. 75 | No. 76 | No. 77
C. 24 (2) | C. 24 (2) | C. 24 (4) | C. 24 (4) | C. 24 (2) | C. 24 (3) | C. 20 (2) | C. 20 (2) | C. 20 (3) | C. 20 (3) | C. 20 (2)

No. 78 | No. 79 | No. 80 | No. 81 | No. 82 | No. 83 | No. 84 | No. 85 | No. 86 | No. 87 | No. 88 | No. 89 | No. 90
C. 18 (4) | C. 18 (4) | C. 18 (5) | C. 18 (3) | C. 18 (4) | C. 18 (4) | C. 18 (4) | C. 18 (4) | C. 18 (3) | C. 18 (2) | C. 16 (2) | C. 16 (2) | C. 16 (3)

No. 91 | No. 92 | No. 93 | No. 94 | No. 95 | No. 96 | No. 97 | No. 98 | No. 99 | No. 100 | No. 101
C. 16 (3) | C. 16 (2) | C. 14 (2) | C. 14 (2) | C. 14 (2) | C. 14 (2) | C. 12 (4) | C. 12 (6) | C. 12 (5) | C. 12 (3) | C 12 (3)

No. 102 | No. 103 | No. 104 | 105 | 106 | No. 107 | No. 108 | No. 109 | No. 110 | No. 111 | No. 112 | No. 113 | No. 114
C. 12 (4) | C. 12 (4) | C. 12 (3) | C. 12 (3) | C. 12 (3) | C. 10 (3) | C. 10 (3) | C. 10 (3) | C. 10 (3) | C. 10 (3) | C. 9 (3) | C. 8 (3) | C. 8 (3)

No. 115 | No. 116 | No. 117 | No. 118 | No. 119 | No. 120 | No. 121 | No. 122 | No. 123 | No. 124
C. 8 (3) | C. 8 (3) | C. 8 (3) | C. 6 (6) | C. 6 (7) | C. 6 (4) | C. 6 (4) | C. 6 (6) | C. 6 (6) | C. 6 (4)

De tusschen haakjes geplaatste cijfers geven het aantal stuks aan dat een minimum van 5 Kg. bevat

Les chiffres placés ( ) indiquent le nombre des pièces dans un minimum de 5 Kg.

N.V. LETTERGIETERIJ „AMSTERDAM" VOORHEEN N. TETTERODE

Border Suggestions

Border Suggestions

SIGRIST-VIGNETTEN

(Galvanos auf Holzfuß)

FREIE VIGNETTEN

(Galvanos auf Holzfuß)

3096

3078

3095

3098

3077

3097

3089

3090

3085

3084

3087

3091

3086

3088

3092

3083

Über 250 Zeichen aller Gebiete des mittelalterlichen Lebens, dazu erläuternden Text, zeigt

DAS ZEICHENBUCH

Die Zeichen sind in der Offenbacher Schreiberwerkstatt in Holz geschnitten.

Verlag Wilhelm Gerstung, Offenbach a. Main

SOLVOLITH

ZAHN STEIN lösende ZAHN PASTA

Hergestellt unter Verwendung von natürlichem Karlsbader Sprudelsalz nach einer gesetzlich geschützten Anweisung von Zahnarzt Dr. med. Karl Hermann. Von ersten Universitäts-Professoren glänzend begutachtet und empfohlen. Solvolith wirkt desinfizierend und macht die Zähne blendend weiß.

FATTINGER-WERKE AKTIENGES. BERLIN NW 7

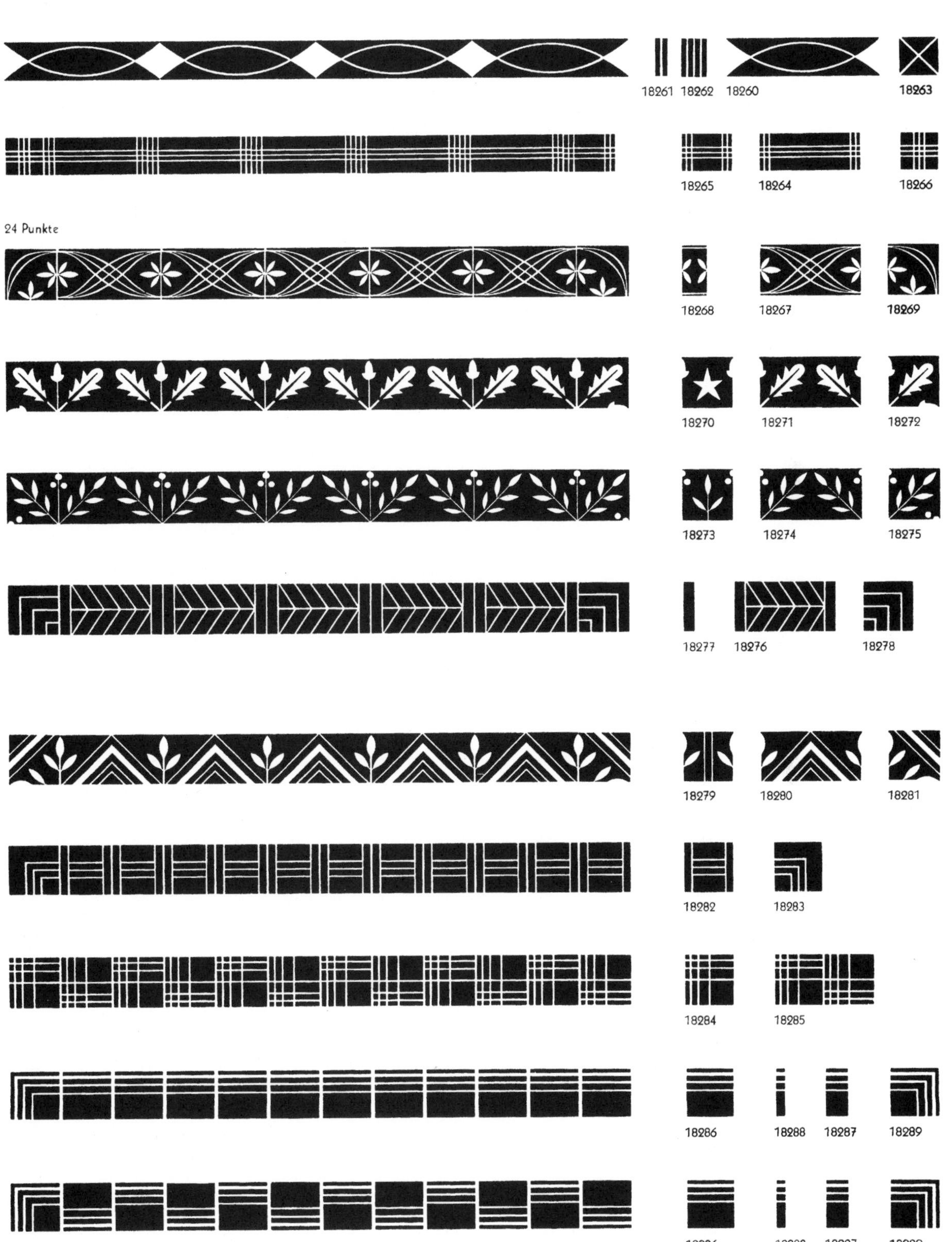
18261 18262 18260 18263
18265 18264 18266
24 Punkte
18268 18267 18269
18270 18271 18272
18273 18274 18275
18277 18276 18278
18279 18280 18281
18282 18283
18284 18285
18286 18288 18287 18289
18286 18288 18287 18289

SIGRIST-EINFASSUNGEN

Sigrist-Vignetten 1188 und 1189

PLAKAT-EINFASSUNGEN

(Schriftguß)

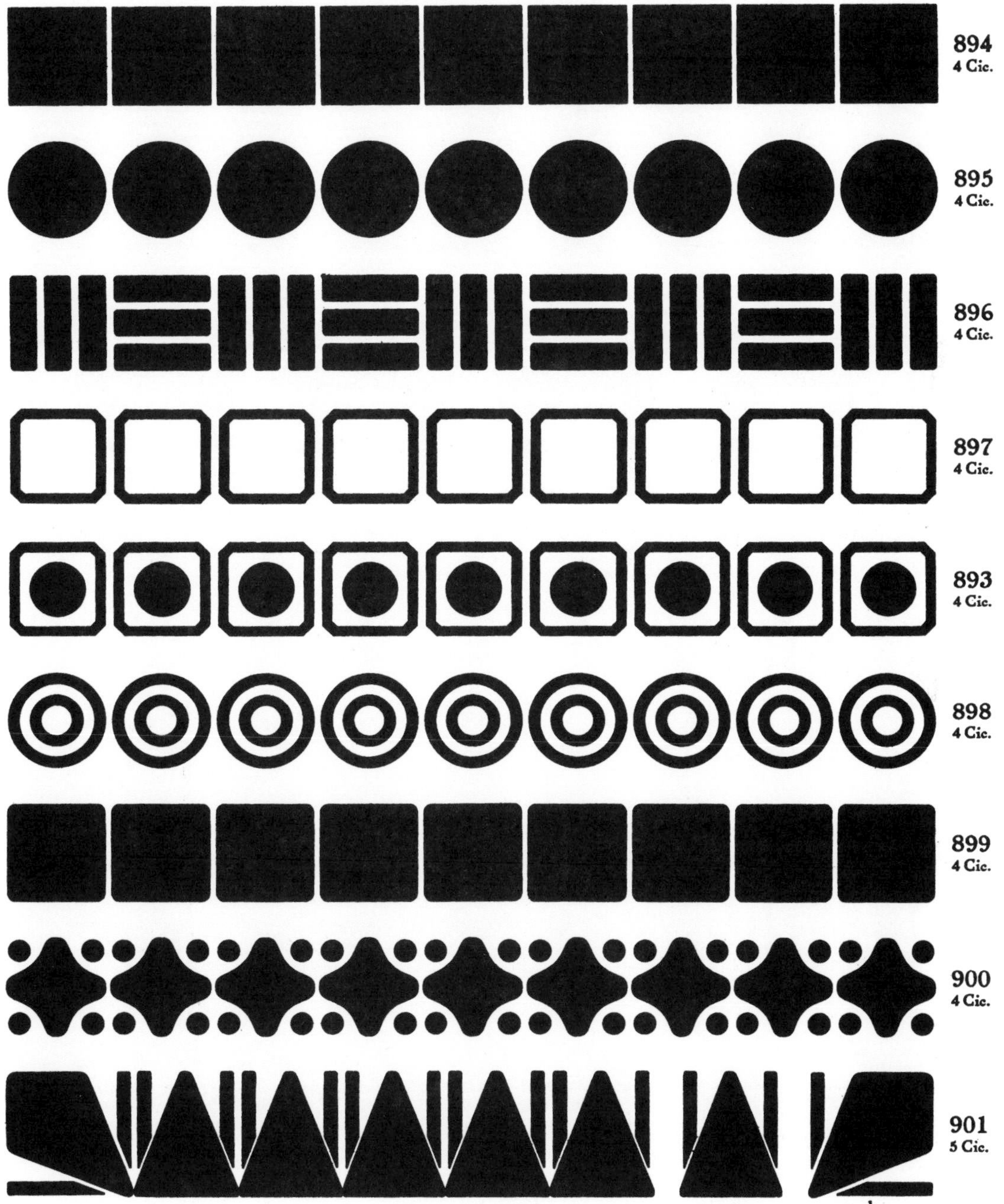

Brüder Butter Dresden

FREGI DI CONTORNO - CORPI 48 E 84

N. 310 **U.** - Corpo 48 - Minimo di ordinazione Kg. 3 a Fr. **6,25** il Kg. Un Metro pesa Kg. 3,600 circa.

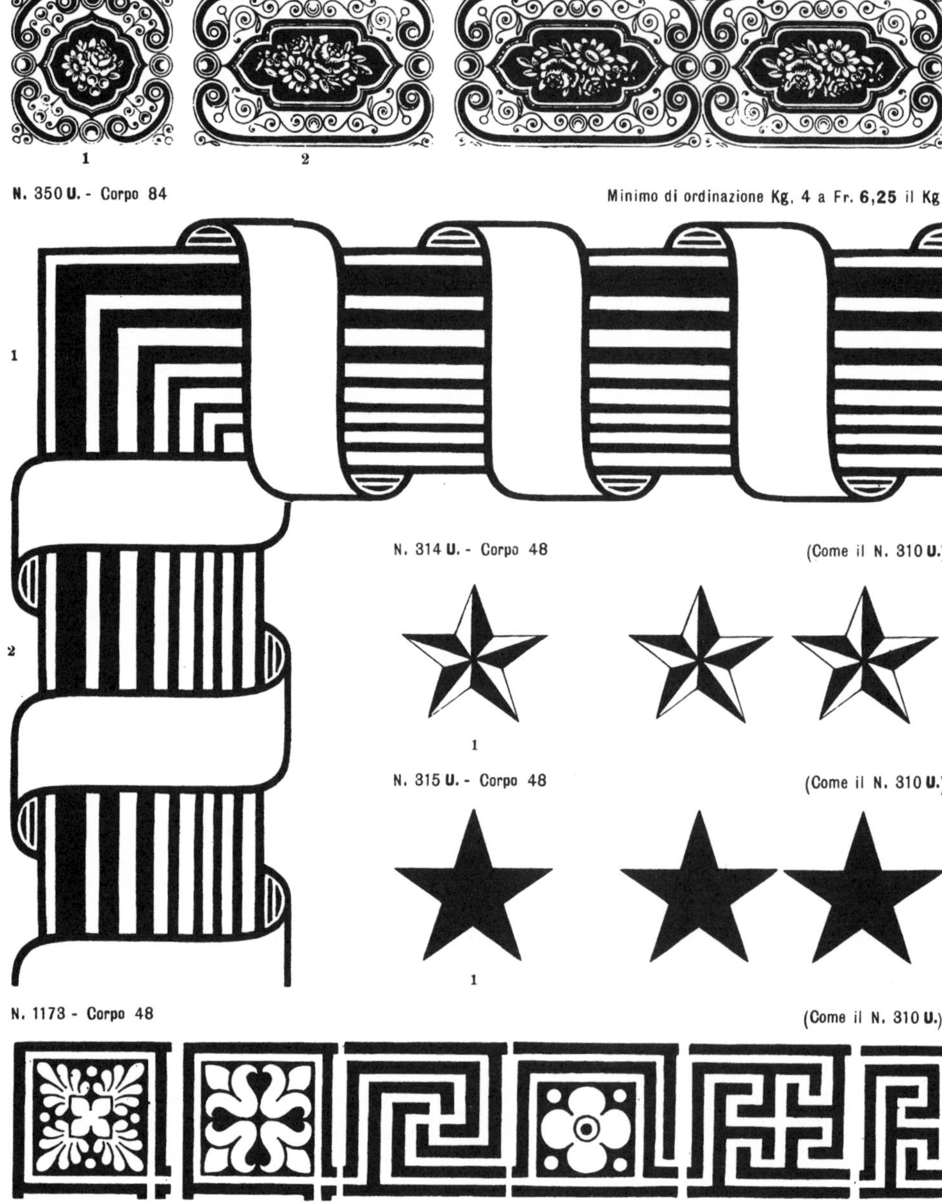

1 2

N. 350 **U.** - Corpo 84 Minimo di ordinazione Kg. 4 a Fr. **6,25** il Kg.

1

2

N. 314 **U.** - Corpo 48 (Come il N. 310 **U.**)

1

N. 315 **U.** - Corpo 48 (Come il N. 310 **U.**)

1

N. 1173 - Corpo 48 (Come il N. 310 **U.**)

1 2 3 4 5 6

SOCIETÀ AUGUSTA TORINO (ITALIA)

FREGI DI CONTORNO - CORPO 48

Minimo di ordinazione Kg. 3 a Fr. **6.25** il Kg. Un Metro pesa Kg. 3.600 circa.

1171 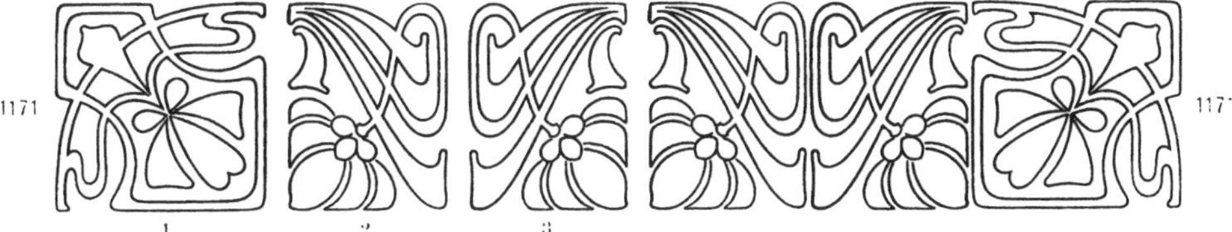 1171

1 2 3

1172     1172

2 1 3

326  326

1 2 3

1174 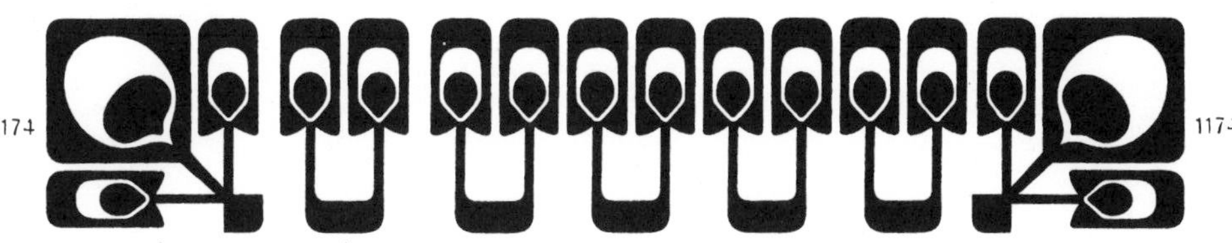 1174

1 2

312 **U.**    312 **U.**

MAZARIN ORNAMENTS NO. 50

UNIQUE BORDERS

Weights and Prices given are Approximate: see page 2.

Two Feet **36 Point Borders** $2\frac{15}{16}$ lbs., **$1.65**

No. 3629

No. 3630

No. 3631

No. 3632

No. 3633

These borders register for color work.

No. 3634

No. 3635

These borders register for color work.

No. 3636

Bordure MÉANDRE, Série N° 4

Collection (388 pièces), **45 fr.** — 1/2 Collection (194 pièces), **25 fr.**

PIÈCES (33 Motifs)

LES ENCOCHES SONT INDIQUÉES EN TEINTE.

Pièces séparées, 8 francs le kilo. — Casseau, 3 francs.

COMPOSITION DE LA COLLECTION :

1563........................	20 Pièces	1566........................	60 Pièces
1561, 1562, 1568, 1569, 1572, 1573, 1574, 1578, 1581	12 —	1570, 1571, 1575, 1576........	10 —
1564, 1567, 1577	16 —	1579, 1580, 1582, 1585, 1586, 1587, 1588, 1589	6 —
1565........................	40 —	1583, 1584, 1590 à 1593.......	4 —

Sorbonne-Initialen

auch zu anderen ähnlichen Charakterschriften passend.

1977. Corps 36. Ein Alphabet M. 22.– einzeln das Stück M. 1.20

1978. Corps 48. Ein Alphabet M. 28.– einzeln das Stück M. 1.50

1979. Corps 60. Ein Alphabet M. 34.—, einzeln das Stück M. 1.75

1980. Corps 72. Ein Alphabet M. 46.—, einzeln das Stück M. 2.50

1981. Corps 96. Ein Alphabet M. 55.—, einzeln das Stück M. 3.—

The Aladdin Ornaments

Font, containing one each Nos. 1, 3, 5, 7, 8, 11 and 15, and two each Nos. 2, 4, 6, 9, 10 and 12, $4.00

No. 1 72-Pt. 35 cts

No. 3 72-Pt. 40 cts

No. 5 72-Pt. 35 cts

No. 7 72-Pt. 35 cts

No. 8 72-Pt. 35 cts

No. 9 72-Pt. 25 cts

No. 10 48-Pt. 20 cts

No. 11 48-Pt. 35 cts

No. 6 48-Pt. 20 cts

No. 2 48-Pt. 20 cts

No. 15 60-Pt. 35 cts

No. 12 24-Pt. 15 cts

No. 4 48-Pt. 20 cts

All Type and Ornaments cast from Superior Copper Alloy Metal

ALADDIN

AND HIS WONDERFUL LAMP

COULD NEVER HAVE BEEN IN IT COMPARED WITH THE RESULTS WHICH MAY BE OBTAINED BY The ALADDIN ORNAMENTS

Made only by

THE H. C. HANSEN TYPE FOUNDRY

Aladdin Ornament No. 12 18 inch font $1.50

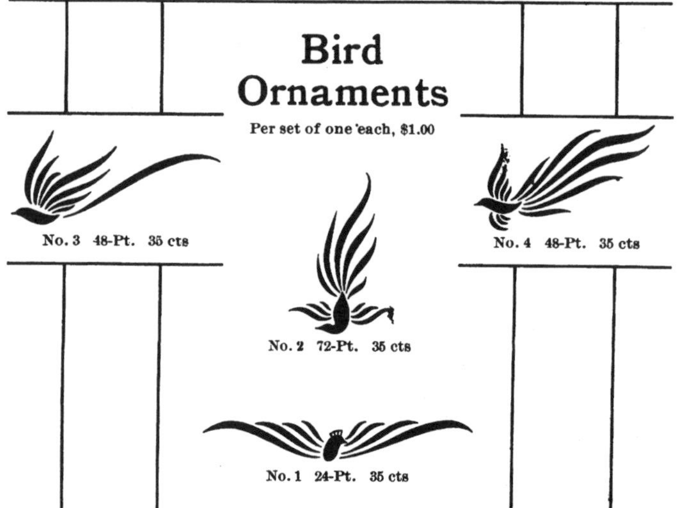

Bird Ornaments

Per set of one each, $1.00

No. 3 48-Pt. 35 cts

No. 4 48-Pt. 35 cts

No. 2 72-Pt. 35 cts

No. 1 24-Pt. 35 cts

A TRUE STORY CONCERNING THE ALADDIN ORNAMENTS

Made by

The H. C. Hansen Type Foundry

Designs Copyrighted

HOLLY ORNAMENTS

Originated by H. C. Hansen

(Electrotypes) Order by Number

No. 323
One color, $1.50
Two colors, $2.75
Mortised

No. 331
Same cut, size 3x3½ in
One color, $1.75
Two colors, $3.25
Mortised

No. 204. $0.75

No. 227. $0.75

No. 321. One color, $1.60
Two colors, $3.00. Mortised

No. 322. Same cut, size 4 ins
One color, $2.00
Two colors, $3.75. Mortised

No. 324. Same cut, size 2 ins
One color, $1.00
Two colors, $1.75 Mortised

No. 326. Same cut, size 1½ ins
One color, $0.75
Two colors, $1.25 Mortised

No. 328
One color, $0.75 Two colors, $1.25
Mortised

No. 329. Same cut, size 2¼x2⅜ inches
One color, $1.00 Two colors, $1.75
Mortised

No. 219. $0.60

No. 228. $1.00
Mortised

No. 203. $0.60

DEBERNY & Cie
BORDURE "MÉANDRE"
Série N° 1 — 29 Motifs
1348
1347
1350
1346 1347 1346
1344 1343
1345
1351
1345 1349 1345
1361
1356 1355
1352
1348 1341 1348

REIHEN-EINFASSUNGEN

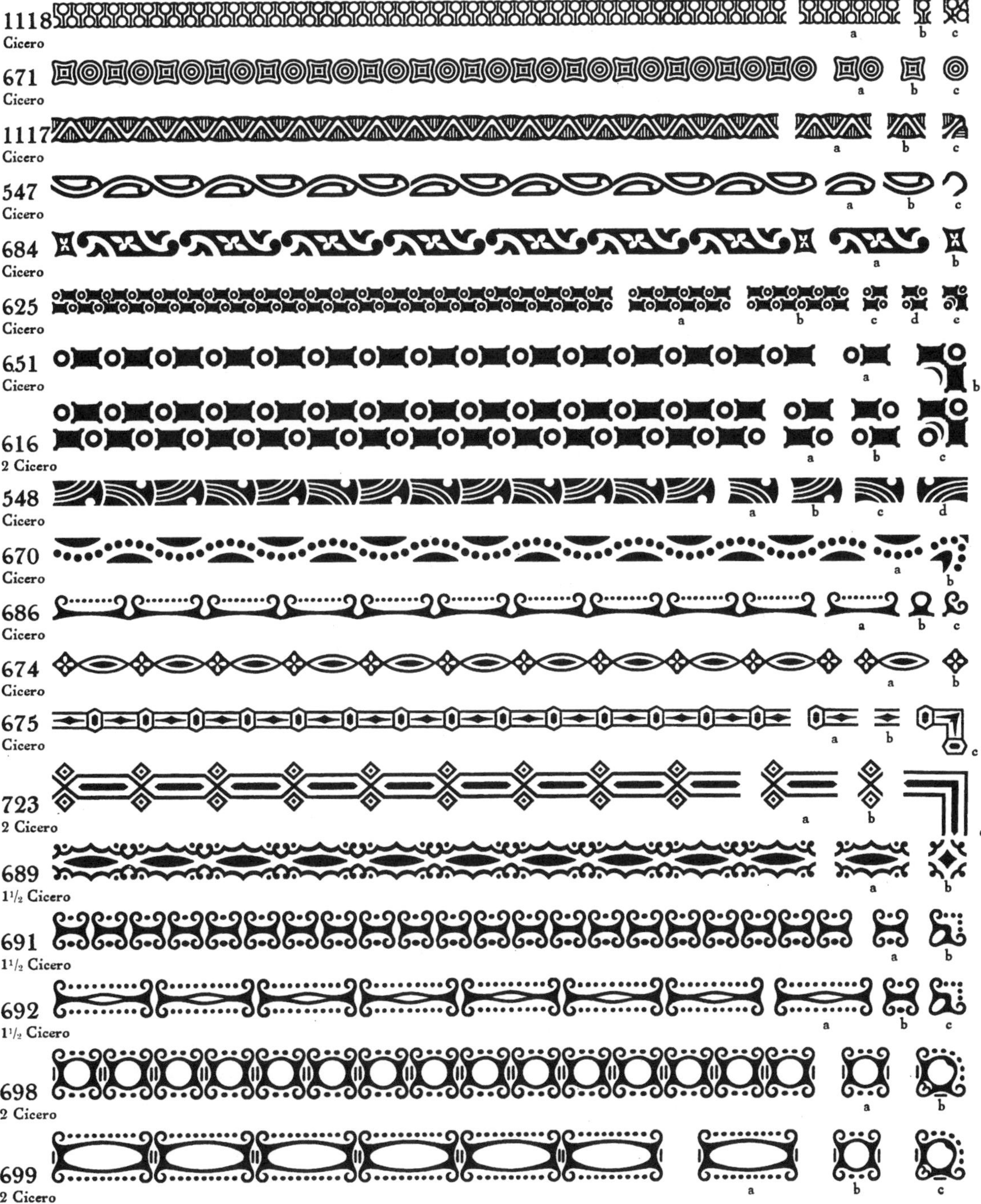

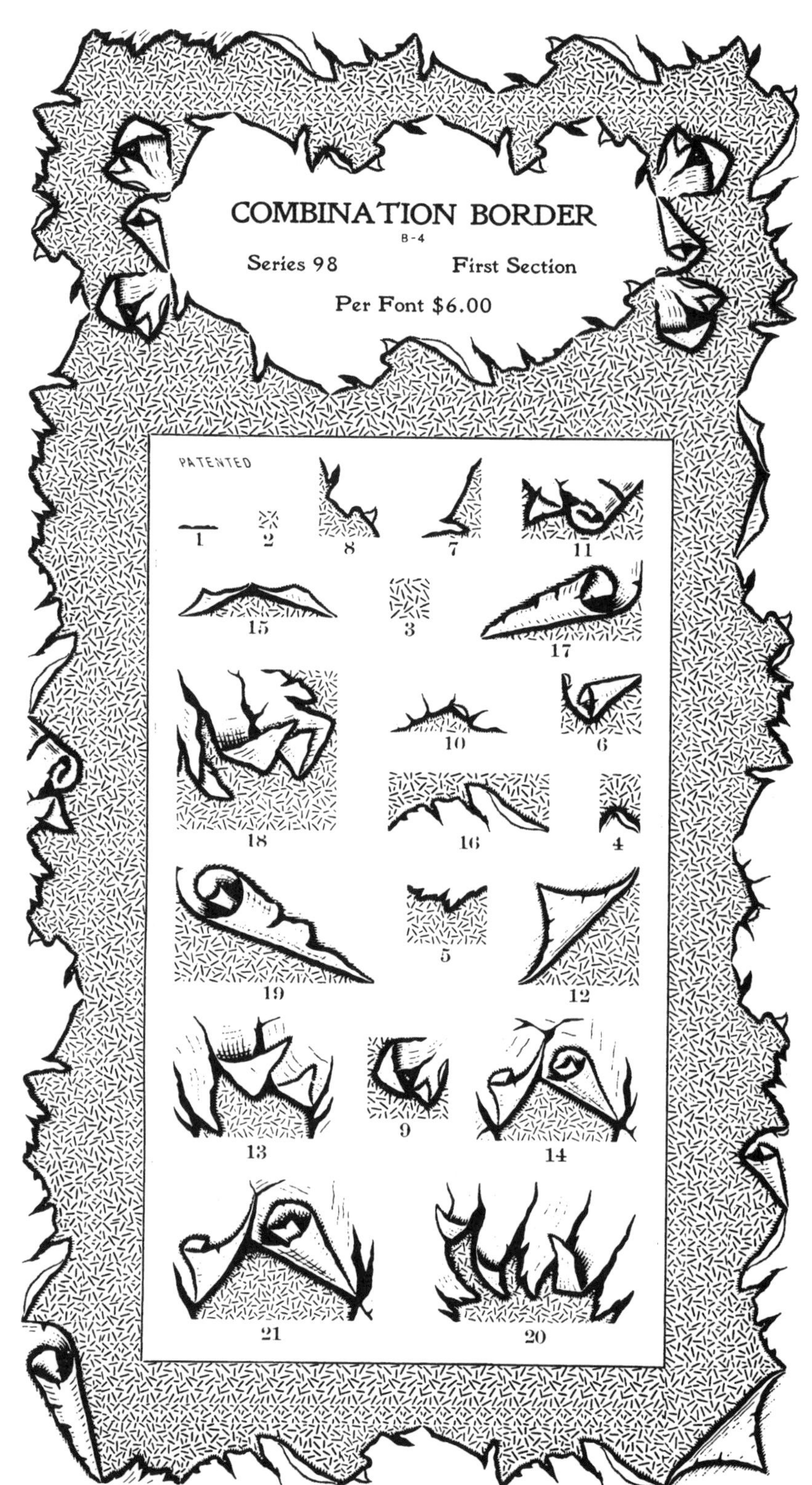
COMBINATION BORDER
B-4
Series 98
First Section
Per Font $6.00
PATENTED
1
2
8
7
11
15
3
17
18
10
6
16
4
19
5
12
13
9
14
21
20

Buchdruckerei Kunstdruckerei
Heinrich Cramer, Offenbach a. M.
Kleinarbeiten aus der Praxis.

Entworfen und gesetzt von P. Dahmen. ◦ Schrift und Empire-Einfassung von Roos & Junge, G. m. b. H., Offenbach a. M. ◦ Papier von Fues & Küstner, Hanau a. M. ◦ Farben: Schramm'sche Lack- und Farbenfabriken, Act.-Ges., Offenbach am Main. ◦ Druck von Heinrich Cramer, Offenbach am Main.

ORIGINAL

Herold-Ornamente Serie 628

GESCHÜTZT

Corps 24. Min. ca. 4 kg

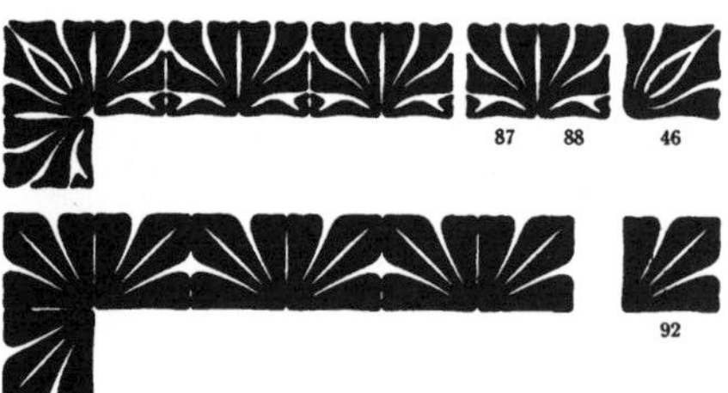

Corps 30. Min. ca. 5 kg

Corps 36. Min. ca. 6 kg

Corps 48. Min. ca. 8 kg

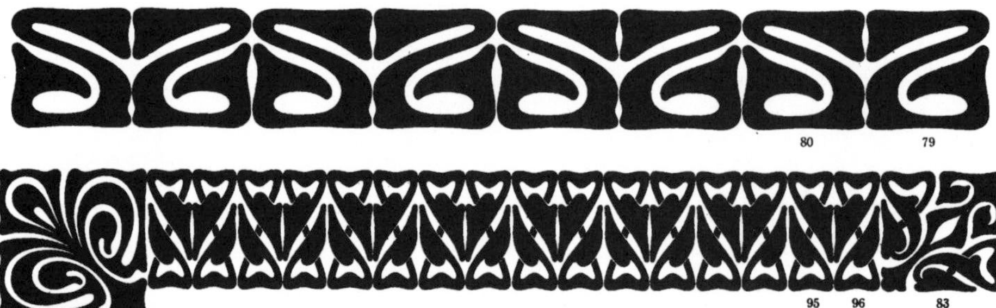

Corps 60. Min. ca. 10 kg

102
103
52
53
78
92
93
79
57
56
75
74
82
50
51
83
85
84
64
65
73
76
68
72
69
77
98
100
101
99

Adornos de bronce
1646
1628
1625
1644
1626
1649
1650
1648
1621
1654
1623
1622
1636
1651
1639
1638
1653
1631
Precios:
Núms. 1625, 1626, 1638, 1644, 1645, 1648 y 1656, Ptas. 3,50 la pieza. Núms. 1631 y 1653, Ptas. 4,50 la pieza. Núms. 1634, 1639, 1642, 1651 y 1652, Ptas. 5,50 la pieza. Núms. 1523, 1627, 1628, 1629, 1635, 1643, 1646, 1650, Ptas 6,50 la pieza. Núms. 1622 y 1649, Ptas. 7,50 la pieza. Núms. 1654, Ptas. 10. Núms. 1621 y 1636, Ptas. 12 la pieza.
En galvanos se sirven estas figuras á mitad de precio.
1642
1645
1656
Estos adornos son de gran efecto en cualquier aplicación; sueltos, combinados con filetes y en medio de cualquier ornamentación, su impresión es fácil y el material es de muchísima duración.
1643
1635
1627
1629
1652

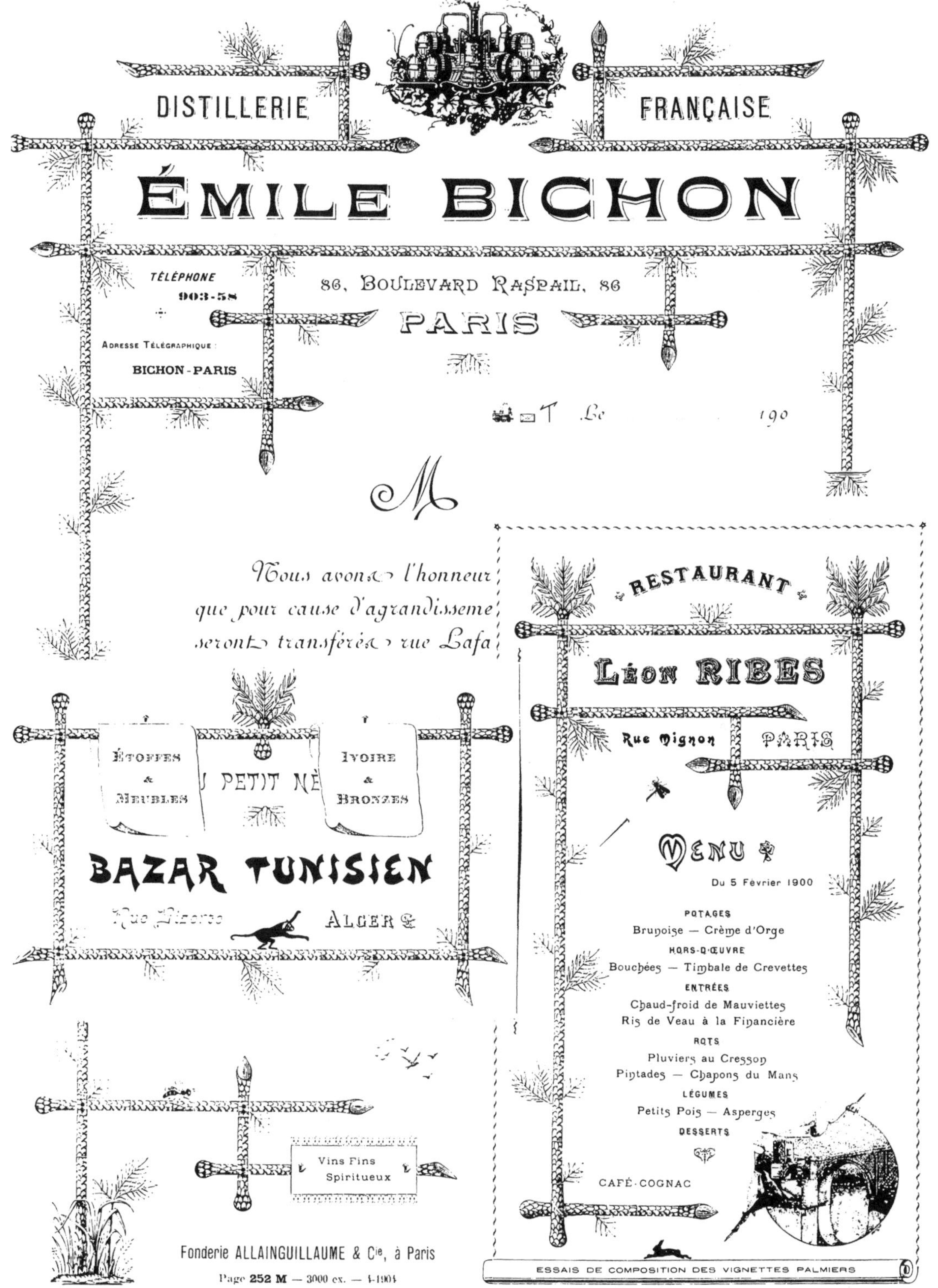
DISTILLERIE
FRANÇAISE
ÉMILE BICHON
TÉLÉPHONE
903-58
86, BOULEVARD RASPAIL, 86
PARIS
ADRESSE TÉLÉGRAPHIQUE :
BICHON-PARIS
Le 190
M
Nous avons l'honneur
que pour cause d'agrandisseme
seront transférés rue Lafa
ÉTOFFES & MEUBLES
IVOIRE & BRONZES
BAZAR TUNISIEN
ALGER
Vins Fins
Spiritueux
Fonderie ALLAINGUILLAUME & Cie, à Paris
Page 252 M — 3000 ex. — 4-1904
RESTAURANT
LÉON RIBES
Rue Mignon
PARIS
MENU
Du 5 Février 1900
POTAGES
Brunoise — Crème d'Orge
HORS-D'ŒUVRE
Bouchées — Timbale de Crevettes
ENTRÉES
Chaud-froid de Mauviettes
Ris de Veau à la Financière
RÔTS
Pluviers au Cresson
Pintades — Chapons du Mans
LÉGUMES
Petits Pois — Asperges
DESSERTS
CAFÉ-COGNAC
ESSAIS DE COMPOSITION DES VIGNETTES PALMIERS

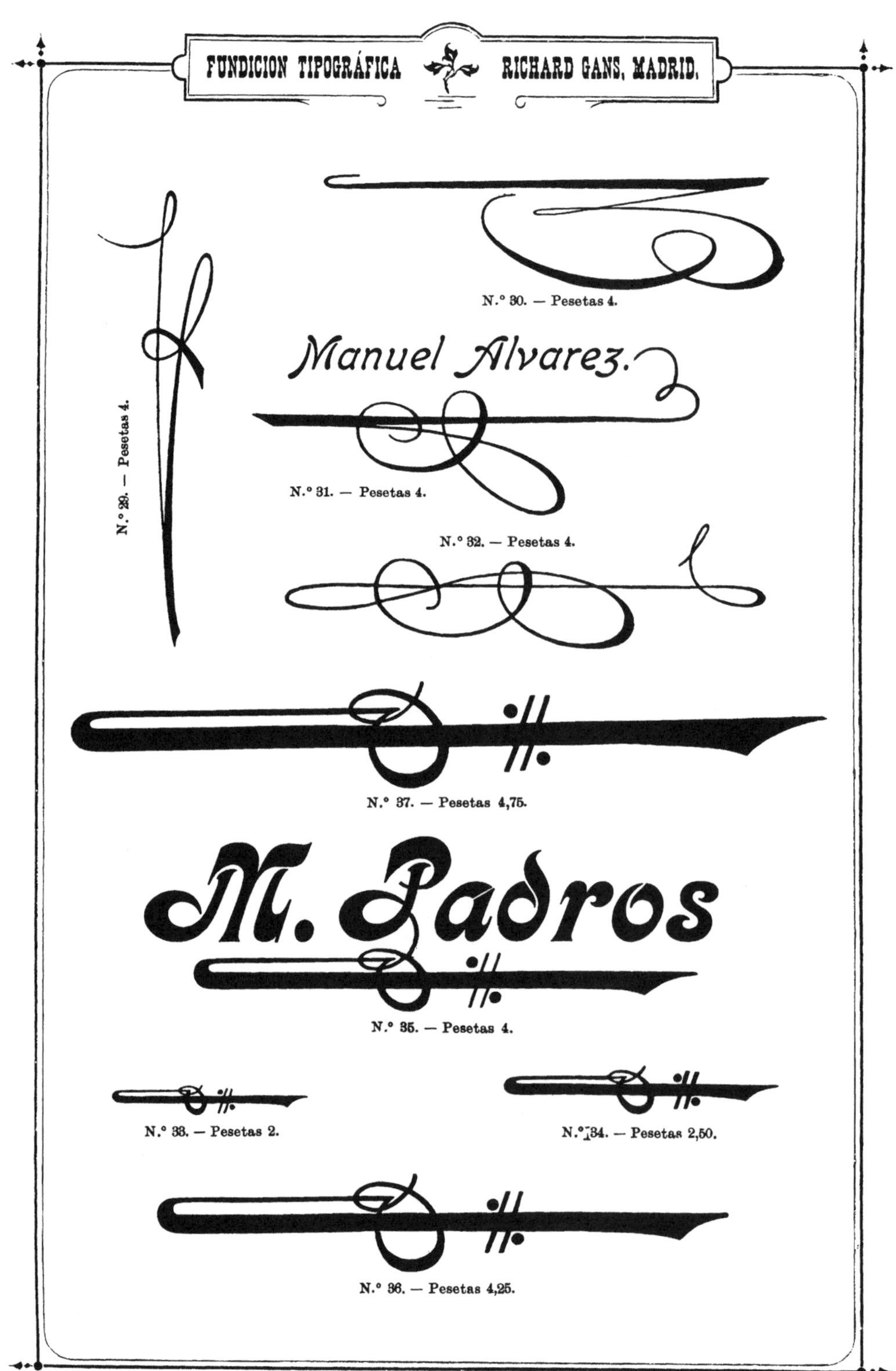
FUNDICION TIPOGRÁFICA RICHARD GANS, MADRID.
N.° 30. — Pesetas 4.
N.° 29. — Pesetas 4.
Manuel Alvarez.
N.° 31. — Pesetas 4.
N.° 32. — Pesetas 4.
N.° 37. — Pesetas 4,75.
M. Padros
N.° 35. — Pesetas 4.
N.° 33. — Pesetas 2.
N.° 34. — Pesetas 2,50.
N.° 36. — Pesetas 4,25.

CUERPO 24

El kilo, Pesetas 7,50. – Un metro pesa cerca de 1,600 kilos.

1

2

3

4

5

6

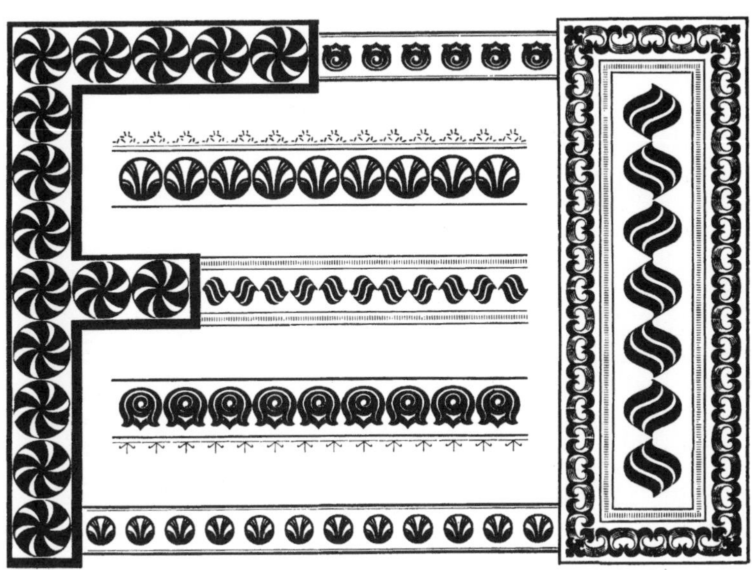

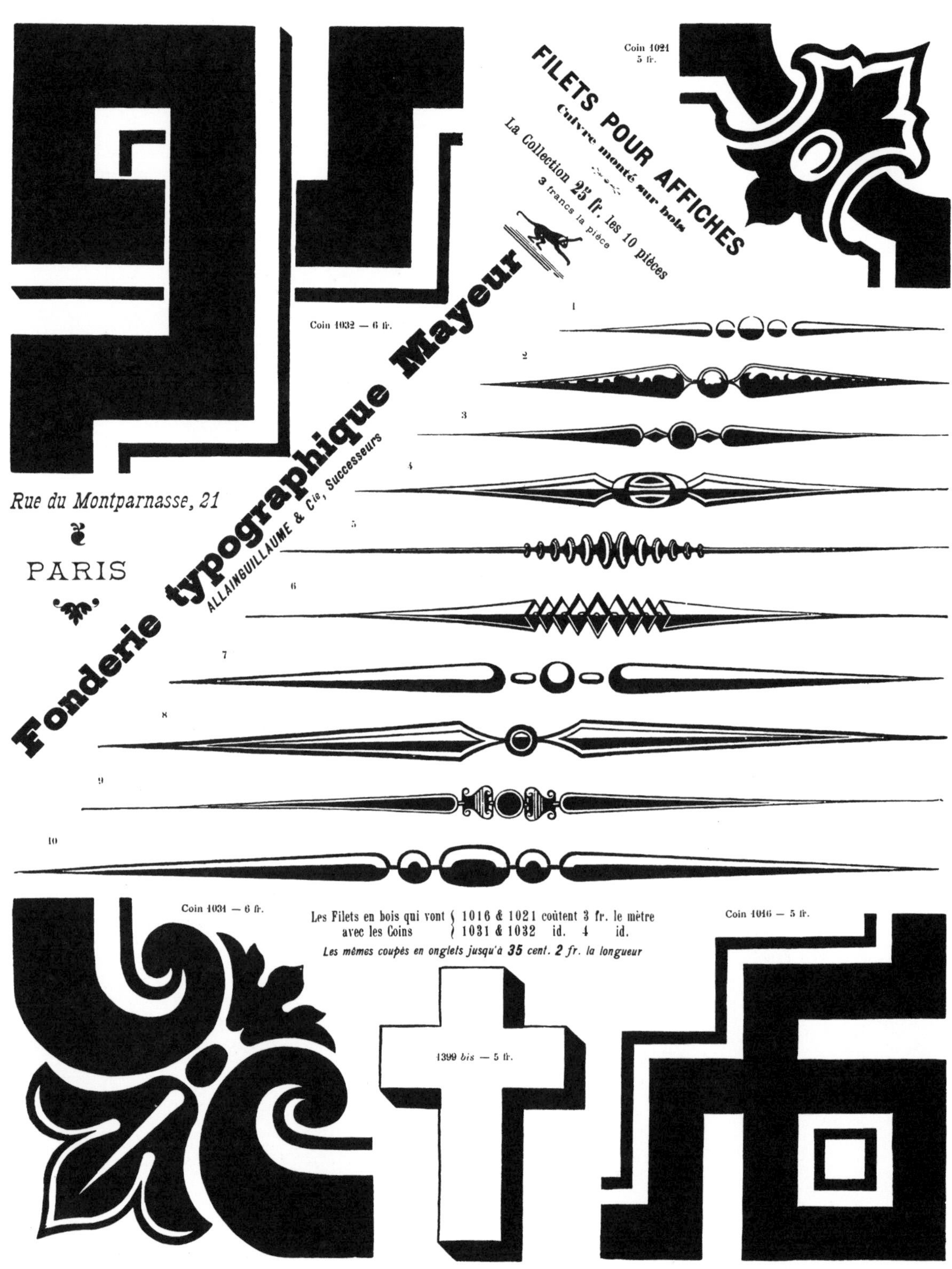

FILETS POUR AFFICHES
Cuivre monté sur bois
La Collection 25 fr. les 10 pièces
3 francs la pièce
Coin 1021
5 fr.
Coin 1032 — 6 fr.
Fonderie typographique Mayeur
ALLAINGUILLAUME & Cie, Successeurs
Rue du Montparnasse, 21
PARIS
1
2
3
4
5
6
7
8
9
10
Coin 1031 — 6 fr.
Les Filets en bois qui vont { 1016 & 1021 coûtent 3 fr. le mètre
avec les Coins { 1031 & 1032 id. 4 id.
Les mêmes coupés en onglets jusqu'à 35 cent. 2 fr. la longueur
Coin 1016 — 5 fr.
1399 bis — 5 fr.
Page 122 M — 3000 exemplaires
2-1904 — ALLAINGUILLAUME & Cie

BASUTO BORDER

The size here shown is Four Line
but other sizes
can be supplied with equal facility

For Prices see
Current Wood Letter Price List

SYNOPSIS

(Four Line)

8 12 8

17 17

9 15

16 5

7

416

Initialen nach Zeichnung von Willi Wegener

No. 75 Guss | Für 1 farbigen Druck: Alphabet M. 30.— Einzelner Buchstabe M. 2.—
Für 2 farbigen Druck: Alphabet M. 45.— Einzelner Buchstabe M. 3.— | corps 48

No. 76 Galvanos | Für 1 farbigen Druck: Alphabet M. 50.— Einzelner Buchstabe M. 2.50
Für 2 farbigen Druck: Alphabet M. 75.— Einzelner Buchstabe M. 3.75 | corps 72

Schriftgießerei Flinsch in Frankfurt am Main

No. 4050|53. corps 36. Satz ca. 4 kg.

4050 4051

4053 ↑ ↑

4052

No. 4054|55. corps 48. Satz ca. 5 kg.

4054 4055

No. 4056. corps 36.

4056

No. 4057|60. corps 48. Satz ca. 5 kg.

4059 4060

Satz ca. 3 kg.

LETTERHEADS

WHO INVENTED STATIONERY? THE HONOR GOES TO THAT UNKNOWN CLERIC OR NOBLE WHO HAND-PRESSED THE first seal on a blank piece of parchment. Nonetheless, the common letterhead was made possible through the advent of the printing press, and further advanced once it was technically possible to print engraved images on paper. Although this does not answer the fundamental question of when, where, or who, it suggests that the letterhead was initially used by the privileged classes, and then, as commercial printing became more affordable, businesses and merchants adopted it. Type specimen books of the early twentieth century were filled with examples of ornate approaches. Designing or composing letterheads and business cards was also the primary service of small printshops. Letterhead design was not viewed within the craft as being on the same level as creating advertising or posters, but given the small space allotted, it certainly was as difficult to compose a bold identity as it was to conceive a grander piece of visual communication.

Letterheads have conformed to the same format for around a century. The typographic design is confined to the "head" of a page, but within that confined space, considerable freedom abounds. Countless lettering possibilities exist as well as numerous graphic options, and color plays a major distinguishing role, too. Unlike a logo or trademark, the letterhead has to both present a "mood" and convey precise information (i.e., name, address, and type of business). Creating pleasing compositions within defined limits has always been the challenge.

MÉDAILLE D'OR PARIS 1900

CARACTÈRES D'IMPRIMERIE

CARACTÈRES
de Fantaisie & Ordinaires

BLANCS · LINGOTS

FILETS
Matière & Cuivre

INTERLIGNES

Choix
de
CLICHÉS
etc.

ALLAINGUILLAUME & Cie

Successeurs de MAYEUR

21, Rue du Montparnasse

(6e Arrondissement)

704-59

PARIS, LE 1905

M

Nous avons l'honneur de vous soumettre nos Écritures Anglaises nouvelles, employées pour Cartes de Visite, Lettres de Mariage et Travaux de ville soignés.

Si quelques-uns de ces Caractères vous convenaient, nous serions très heureux d'être favorisés de vos ordres.

Veuillez agréer, Monsieur, nos bien sincères et empressées salutations.

Allainguillaume & Cie

Écriture anglaise corps 30 n° 5 (petit œil)
15 fr. le kilo

Page **313 M** — 5700 ex.

3-1905 — DÉPOSÉ

Applications Générales de l'Électricité dans l'Industrie

BARTHÉLEMY

BREVETÉ S.G.D.G.

Télégraphie
Acoustique
Sonneries
Téléphonie
Piles

Suspensions
Flambeaux
Réflecteurs
Appliques
Lampes

23, Rue de la Canebière & Rue de la République, 42

MARSEILLE

Grands Magasins de Nouveautés

Msons MOLIÈRE & DAUBENTON Réunies

AU PRINTEMPS

Confections
Trousseaux
Layettes

35, *Avenue Parmentier*

Comptoir
d'Ameublement
Tentures riches
& Tapis

TÉLÉPHONE
603-58

MEAUX

"ORNEMENTS ALGÉRIENS" DE LA FONDERIE ALLAINGUILLAUME & Cie, PARIS

THE ROOSEVELT

NEW ORLEANS LOUISIANA, U.S.A.

SEYMOUR WEISS
PRESIDENT AND
MANAGING DIRECTOR

JAS. (PAT) O'SHAUGHNESSY
VICE PRESIDENT AND
GENERAL MANAGER

CABLE ADDRESS
"HOROSEVELT" NEW ORLEANS

Bel-Air

OWNED BY THE
ALPHONZO E. BELL CORPORATION

SALES OFFICE:
ADMINISTRATION BUILDING, BEL-AIR

LOS ANGELES, CALIFORNIA
10601 CHALON ROAD, TELEPHONE OXFORD 1175

Litefut
SHOES

MAIN STREET BOOT SHOP

AUTHORIZED "LITEFUT" DEALER

MAIN STREET AT ELM, DALLAS, OKLA.

CREDIT OFFICE

New York

RICKARD & WARD

793 WALNUT STREET MILWAUKEE

Hat Manufacturers

N·L·PAGE & SON CO·

MANUFACTURERS OF

Game Tables and Toys

NEW YORK OFFICE
ROOM 416 FIFTH AVE. BLDG.

AUBURN·MAINE

☆ KNITWEAR

☆ SPORTSWEAR

BENDIX

Home Appliances, Inc.

DETROIT · · BRANCH
5402 SECOND BLVD. · DETROIT

WILBUR & THOMAS FERTILIZER CO.

Manufacturers of EXCEL Fertilizer Dealers in All Agricultural Chemicals

GREENVILLE · OHIO

STORAGE, MOVING, PACKING, SHIPPING

Robert
STORAGE COMPANY

WAREHOUSES • 717 CAMPBELL STREET • 30 NORTH CLIFTON AVENUE
ALL TELEPHONES • CLIFTON 8723
KENNERLY, CALIFORNIA

BAGS AND TRAVELING

LEFFINGWELL
LEATHER GOODS COMPANY
1220 West Sheldrake Avenue, Munising, Michigan

The Philadelphia Bindery Inc.

VINE STREET AT THIRD · PHILADELPHIA

PAMPHLETS · FOLDERS · WIRE-O · PLASTIC AND INVISO BINDING

ALCONA • MANUFACTURING

ALCONA WOODEN SPECIALTIES • GARDEN FURNISHINGS

MILL ON RIDGLEY ROAD, PARNEL, VERMONT

SINCE 1919

ACME-SWARTZ SIGNS

VERNON 7890

709 PENNSYLVANIA AVENUE

GRILLS GATES SIGNS RAILINGS

14 FERRY STREET TEL. MALDEN 209

SHIELDS

WROUGHT IRON WORK

SHEFFIELD, ILLINOIS

TRADEMARKS

THE COMMERCIAL LOGO DATES BACK TO MEDIEVAL TIMES. THE COUSIN OF ARISTOCRATIC SHIELDS AND COATS OF ARMS, it was a device used by merchants to identify their respective wares. Gradually, the form evolved into brands that distinguished one business from another. Ultimately, trademarks identified different products, as well. These marks had to be simple, graphic, and memorable—clarity was key. And by the early twentieth century, trademarks were comprised of virtually every fundamental graphic element, including drawing, type, geometric and abstract shapes, and combinations thereof. Most trademarks are customized to represent a specific concern, yet various type and printing specimen books that were published during the early twentieth century offered iterations that could be universally applied. These "generic" trademarks are not void of imagination but rather serve as models for those who are. Although some "ready-to-use" marks rely on stereotypical imagery to represent specific trades or products, others provide stylistic options applicable for diverse purposes.

Before the advent of high-priced corporate identity firms, most small, and even large businesses were fairly lackadaisical about the design of their trademarks. A few leaders stood out for having unmistakable, in fact, progressive logos, but the majority of the world's industries found that it was unnecessary for these *aides de memoire* to be entirely original to be effective. In fact, trademarks with familiar imagery offer greater opportunities to tickle the consciousness, at least in the short term, than those untried.

TRADE MARK SUGGESTIONS

10

TRADE MARK SUGGESTIONS

TRADE MARK SUGGESTIONS

TRADE MARK SUGGESTIONS

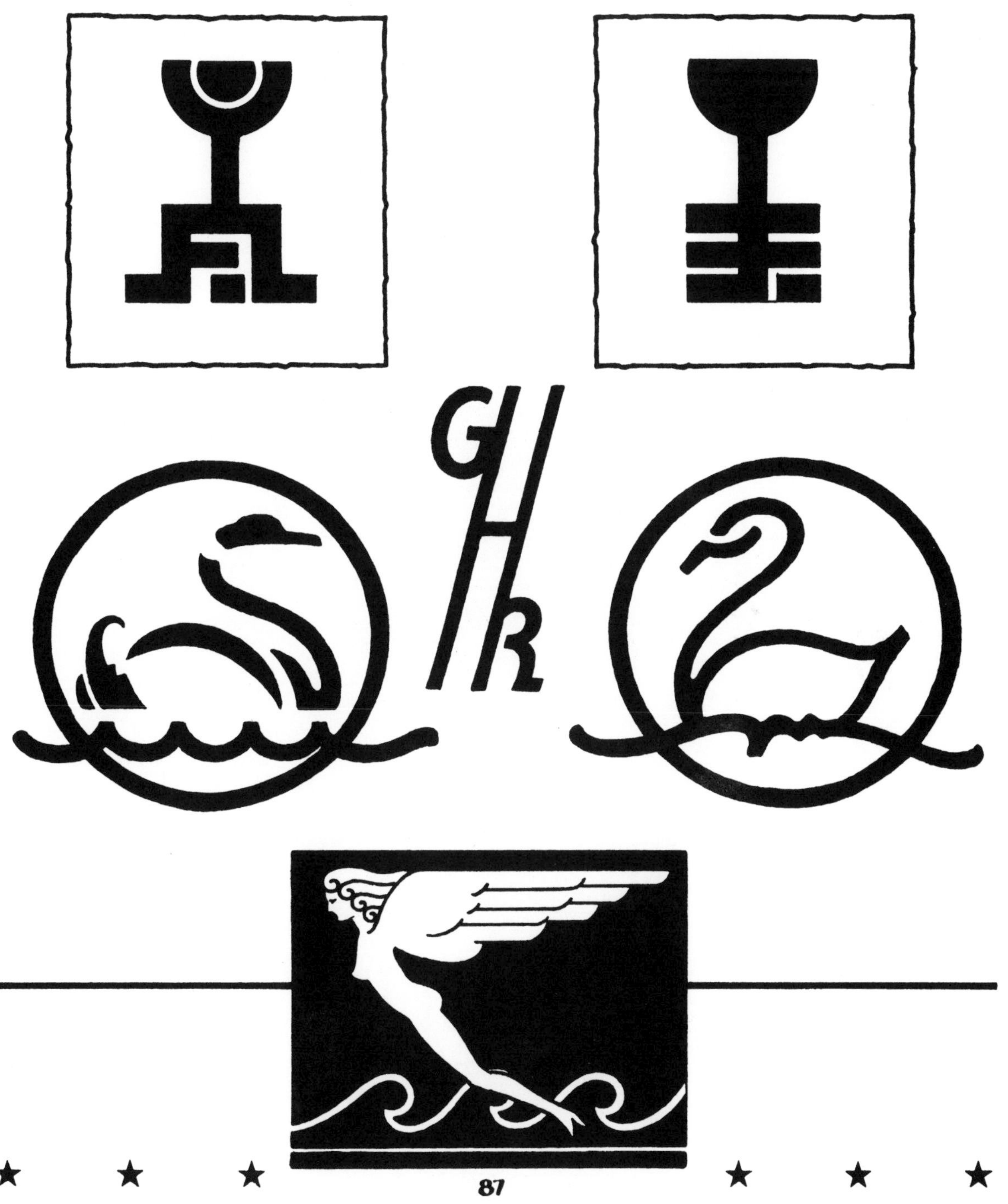

87

MOLKEREI
OSTHAFEN
GMBH

PHELPS'
HOME MADE
MAYONNAISE
32 FLD. OZ.
BATAVIA
N.Y.

BUY AT THIS SIGN
PENZBEST
REG.NO 216831
KENDALL
Guaranteed
100% PURE
PENNSYLVANIA
OIL
PERMIT No 3
MOTOR OILS
IT IS YOUR PROTECTION